LIVING THROUGH THE GULF WARS WITH IRAQ

D0641996

Jane Bingham

Heinemann LIBRARY

Chicago, Illinois

www.capstonepub.com
Visit our website to find out more information about Heinemann-Raintree books.

To order:
☎ Phone 888-454-2279
💻 Visit www.capstonepub.com
  to browse our catalog and order online.

© 2012 Heinemann Library
an imprint of Capstone Global Library, LLC
Chicago, Illinois

Edited by Andrew Farrow, Adam Miller, and Vaarunika Dharmapala
Designed by Steve Mead
Original illustrations © Capstone Global Ltd 2012
Illustrations by Jeff Edwards
Picture research by Ruth Blair
Originated by Capstone Global Library Ltd
Printed and bound in the USA

15 14 13 12 11
10 9 8 7 6 5 4 3 2 1

Library of Congress Cataloging-in-Publication Data
Bingham, Jane.
  The Gulf wars with Iraq / Jane Bingham.
    p. cm.—(Living through...)
  Includes bibliographical references and index.
   ISBN 978-1-4329-5997-5 (hb)—ISBN 978-1-4329-6006-3 (pb) 1. Persian Gulf War, 1991—Juvenile literature. 2. Iraq War, 2003—Juvenile literature. I. Title.
   DS79.723.B46 2012
   956.7044'2—dc22   2011015922

Acknowledgments
We would like to thank the following for permission to reproduce photographs: akg-images pp. 9 (RIA Novosti), 52 (ullstein bild); Corbis pp. 12 (© Stringer/Iraq/Reuters), 17 (© Pool/Reuters), 29, 57 (© Reuters), 30 (© Rick Maiman/Sygma), 37 (© David Turnley), 41 (© Peter Turnley), 43 (© Alexandra Boulat/VII), 51 (© Ron Haviv/VII), 59 (© Handout/CNP), 61 (© Wathiq Khuzaie/Pool/epa), 64 (© Mohammed Ameen/Reuters); Getty Images pp. 10 (Hulton Archive), 15 (Alex Bowie), 19 (Kaveh Kazemi), 20 (Emory Kristof/National Geographic), 23 (Ron Sachs/CNP), 26 (Time Life Pictures/Time & Life Pictures), 32 (Consolidated News Pictures), 34 (MPI), 45 (Karim Sahib/AFP), 49 (Chip Somodevilla); Photolibrary p. 39 (Oxford Scientific).

Cover photograph reproduced with the permission of Corbis (© Khalil Al-A'Ani/epa).

Every effort has been made to contact copyright holders of any material reproduced in this book. Any omissions will be rectified in subsequent printings if notice is given to the publisher.

CONTENTS

Words printed in **bold** are explained in the glossary.

WAR IN THE GULF

Between 1990 and today, two major wars have been waged in the southern region of the Persian Gulf. The First Gulf War was fought in Kuwait and Iraq, and it lasted from August 1990 to February 1991. The Second Gulf War, which is often simply known as the Iraq War, has been fought almost entirely in Iraq. It began in 2003 and reached its final stages in 2010, when the last combat troops left Iraq.

TWO GULF WARS

During the First Gulf War, the Iraqi army faced a military **coalition** (group of forces from several nations) made up of soldiers from 34 countries. The Coalition was led by the United States, and it aimed to expel Iraqi troops that had invaded the kingdom of Kuwait. This aim was achieved in just seven months.

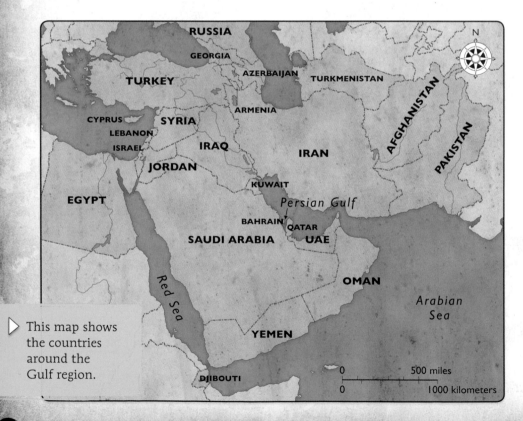

▷ This map shows the countries around the Gulf region.

In 2003, a much smaller coalition, led once again by the United States, embarked on the Second Gulf War. This time the aim was to remove President Saddam Hussein from power in Iraq. In less than a month, Coalition troops had seized control of the Iraqi capital and Saddam had gone into hiding. But this was just the start of a long and violent struggle to control and rebuild a shattered country.

A GLOBAL IMPACT

Conflict in the Gulf has a major impact on the wider world. This is partly because the region is very rich in oil. All of the world's industrialized nations need oil in order to function, so their leaders are anxious to have an influence in the Gulf.

The nations of the Gulf are all Arab countries with a mainly Muslim population. Since the attacks on the World Trade Center and the Pentagon on September 11, 2001, some dangerous tensions have developed between Muslims of the Arab world and Western nations, especially the United States. These tensions have been an underlying factor throughout the Second Gulf War.

LOOKING AT THE WARS

This book addresses challenging issues. How did troops from the United States and United Kingdom become so deeply involved in the region? What led the Coalition to invade for a second time? Why is it taking so long for Iraq to find peace, given that a brutal dictator has been overthrown? And why has there been so much controversy surrounding the war?

Many names

The wars in the Gulf have been given several different names. The First Gulf War is often simply called the Gulf War. It is also sometimes known as Operation Desert Storm, even though that term applies only to the first stage of the Coalition's operations. In the Middle East, the First Gulf War was called the "Liberation of Kuwait," while Saddam Hussein named it the "Mother of All Battles." The Second Gulf War is often known as the Iraq War.

SADDAM'S IRAQ

The central figure in both Gulf Wars was Iraq's brutal dictator, Saddam Hussein. Saddam first rose to power in 1968, when he was made deputy president of Iraq. For the next 10 years, he held the post of deputy under President al-Bakr.[1] In fact, al-Bakr was little more than a figurehead, while Saddam worked tirelessly to bring the country under his personal control.

A DIVIDED LAND

The country Saddam took over in 1968 had enormous problems. Iraq had only existed as a nation for 50 years, having been created by the British after World War I (see box), and throughout its history it had proved very hard to govern. Large areas of Iraq were desert lands, ruled by rival nomadic tribes, but the nation also contained some modern cities, such as Baghdad, Basra, and Mosul. The Iraqi people were deeply divided between nomadic tribes of the desert and city dwellers. There were also bitter divisions between rival religious and racial groups.

Within Iraq there were three main regions. In the north were the **Kurds**. In the marshlands of the south were the Arab **Shi'a** Muslims, and in the center were the Arab **Sunni** Muslims. These three groups had been locked in conflict for centuries. But after the creation of Iraq, they were forced to see themselves as members of one nation.

A STRUGGLE FOR OIL

The other key element in Iraq's troubled history was oil. Significant sources of oil were first discovered in 1927 and divided among the British, the French, the Dutch, and the Americans, with the United Kingdom gaining the greatest share. It was not until 1972 that the Iraqis finally managed to gain control of their own oil.[2]

Iraq before Saddam

The country now known as Iraq was created in 1921. Before then, it had been ruled by Turkey as part of the vast **Ottoman** Empire. Following Turkey's defeat in World War I (1914–18) by the United Kingdom and its allies, the British took control of some of the Ottoman lands around the Persian Gulf, drawing up the boundaries of the new nation of Iraq. For the first 11 years of its existence Iraq was a "British mandate," a nation under the special protection of the UK government. The British chose an Arab monarch to rule the country, and UK forces were kept stationed in Iraq.

In 1932, Iraq was declared to be an independent kingdom, but the British remained in charge behind the scenes, still controlling the monarch and maintaining a military presence in the country. In 1958, however, the Iraqi army finally seized control of the country. It set up an independent **republic**, banishing the royal family and expelling all UK troops. For the next 11 years, the Republic of Iraq was ruled by a series of **military dictators**. These men struggled to maintain control of their divided people up until the time that Saddam came to power.[3]

SADDAM'S AIMS

Saddam belonged to the **Ba'ath Party**, a strongly left-wing political party that first gained power in Iraq in the early 1960s. The Ba'athists wanted to create a more equal, modern society in Iraq, modeled on the communist system of the Soviet Union. Most Ba'ath party members were Sunni Muslims (like Saddam), and their party was opposed to the extreme religious practices favored by many Shi'ites. They were also passionate Arab **nationalists**, who wished to free all Arab nations from control by Western countries.

In his role as "Mr. Deputy," Saddam worked hard to bring Iraq into the modern age. He wanted Iraq to be a **secular** society, in which religion did not dominate people's lives, and in which women could be part of the workforce. In many ways this was an admirable project. But Saddam used some extremely ruthless methods to achieve it.

Kurds, Sunnis, and Shi'as

The major conflicts within Iraq are between the rival **ethnic** groups of the Kurds and the Arabs, and the rival religious groups of the Sunni and Shi'a Muslims. The Kurds represent just 15 percent of the country's population.[4] They belong to a race of people who have lived for centuries in the area now covered by northern Iraq, as well as parts of Iran, Syria, and Turkey. The Iraqi Kurds strongly resent being ruled by Arabs, and they have been campaigning for an independent state ever since the creation of Iraq in the 1920s. Most Kurds are Sunni Muslims, but although they share their religious views with Arab Sunnis, they still fight against them for independence.

The Sunnis and Shi'as belong to rival groups within the Muslim faith. Their split dates back to the 7th century, when the followers of the Prophet Muhammad argued over who was his rightful heir, meaning who should take over. Traditionally, the Sunnis have belonged to the ruling class, even though they make up just 35 percent of Iraqi Muslims.[5]

MONEY AND POWER

Saddam's social reforms were paid for by money from oil. One of his first moves was to nationalize (put into government ownership) the Iraq Petroleum Company, which had previously been owned by a group of Western countries. With Iraq's oil resources under his control, Saddam was in an immensely powerful position. Western leaders were unwilling to criticize his government, worried that he could stop their supply of oil.

△ From 1969 to 1979, Saddam (on the right) was known as "Mr. Deputy," but he was really in charge of everything that went on in Iraq. He is seen here with Alexei Kosygin, a senior Soviet statesman.

FOREIGN FRIENDS

During Saddam's years as "Mr. Deputy," Iraq made powerful foreign friends. The Iraqi government forged strong links with other Arab countries, joining with them to support the cause of Arab nationalism. Iraq also formed a close **alliance** (friendship) with the Soviet Union.

In the 1970s, there was a "cold war," with the Soviet Union on one side and the United States and the United Kingdom on the other. The United States and United Kingdom saw Iraq's friendship with the Soviet Union as a serious threat to their security. They were especially afraid that the Soviets might block the supply of oil from Iraq to the West.

SOCIAL IMPROVEMENTS

In the 1970s, Saddam impressed the world with his program for social improvement. Free schools were set up across Iraq to teach a modern curriculum to both boys and girls, and a national campaign was introduced to teach all Iraqis to read. Saddam's government funded new roads and public housing. Hospital treatment was free for all, and the Iraqi public health system became one of the best in the Middle East. Electricity was brought to nearly every city, and agriculture was modernized. However, all these improvements were achieved at a terrible cost to the Iraqi people.

A RULE OF TERROR

While the world admired Saddam's reforms, few outsiders had any idea of the dark side of life in Iraq. The country was controlled by an inner circle of ruthless operators who all answered directly to Saddam. Many were members of his family. These powerful figures, who belonged to the Sunni branch of Islam, followed Saddam's example in their cruel suppression of other elements of Iraqi society.

By the 1970s, Iraqis had learned to obey all government demands and never to criticize Saddam. Any sign of protest was punished by instant imprisonment, by brutal torture, and often by death. There were government spies everywhere, and even silence or a stare could result in arrest or execution.

△ This picture of Saddam Hussein was taken in 1970.

Saddam used a range of methods to keep control of the Iraqi people. The Iraqi army was responsible for appalling massacres, especially of the Kurds (see pages 16 to 19). The People's Army cracked down on any uprisings within the army, while the Department of General Intelligence (known in Iraq as Mukhabarat) spied on Iraqi citizens. Mukhabarat officers were widely feared because of their use of torture to extract false confessions from innocent people.

In 1979, Saddam forced President al-Bakr to resign and became the new president of Iraq. This move was followed by a violent display of power. Saddam claimed that many members of the Ba'ath Party were involved in anti-government plots, and, within a few weeks, hundreds of senior party members had been executed. Once he was president, Saddam felt free to rule even more harshly than before.

BIOGRAPHY

Saddam Hussein, 1937–2006
BORN: al-Awja, central Iraq
ROLE: Deputy president of Iraq, 1968–1979
President of Iraq, 1979–2003

Saddam Hussein came from a poor, rural background. His father had either died or left Saddam's mother before his son was born. Saddam's mother remarried, but Saddam was harshly treated by his stepfather, and when he was about 10 years old he escaped to Baghdad to live with his uncle. As a young man, Saddam was a passionate supporter of the Ba'ath Party. In 1959 he was involved in an unsuccessful plot to **assassinate** the ruler of Iraq. In 1964 he was imprisoned, but he escaped three years later. In 1968 the Ba'ath Party came to power, and the following year Saddam was made deputy president of Iraq. Ten years later, he became president. In public, Saddam's image was presented as a smiling father of his people, but this kindly mask disguised his real personality as a cruel and violent dictator, who was determined to hang on to power at any cost. Saddam led his country in the Iran-Iraq War (1980–1988) and in the two Gulf Wars. He was captured in December 2003, eight months after the fall of Baghdad. An Iraqi court sentenced him to death by hanging.[6]

DID YOU KNOW? After becoming president, Saddam had several "doubles" who pretended to be him on formal occasions. Saddam used these doubles to give his people the impression that he was "everywhere," watching whatever they did.

LIFE UNDER SADDAM

△ After he became president in 1979, Saddam made sure that no one could ignore his presence. Thousands of posters, portraits, statues, and murals of Saddam appeared all over Iraq.

In the years following the fall of Saddam, some shocking stories emerged about life under his rule. Saddam's spies were everywhere, and his secret police were ready to pounce on anyone who dared to criticize him. His people lived in constant fear of arrest, imprisonment, torture, and even death.

MAYADA'S STORY

Mayada Al-Askari was the owner of a small print shop in Baghdad. One morning, three strangers burst into her office. After searching the print shop, they bundled her into their car and drove her straight to prison. She was accused of the crime of printing anti-Saddam pamphlets.

Mayada had never printed any political pamphlets, but she was tortured to make her "confess." Wires were fixed to her toe and ear and electric shocks were passed through her body. When Mayada fainted with pain, she was taken to a crowded, dirty cell, which she shared with 17 other innocent women. They all faced the same treatment: torture and the threat of execution if they did not "confess" to their crimes.

After three weeks in prison, Mayada was released, but she never knew why she was suddenly granted her freedom. She later managed to escape from Iraq and wrote about her experiences in the book *Mayada: Daughter of Iraq.*[7]

AN ATMOSPHERE OF FEAR

Nobody was safe from Saddam. He was even capable of suddenly turning against one of his favorites. The daughter of Saddam's personal pilot, Zainab Salbi, wrote a revealing account of her childhood spent within Saddam's small circle of staff and "admirers."[8] Salbi describes agonizing times spent in Saddam's company, trying to please him in every way. In order to keep safe, she learned to match her response to his. If he was serious, she was serious, and if he smiled, she smiled—even when she was being told of the death of somebody she knew.

SADDAM THE CHILDREN'S FRIEND?

All children in Iraq were encouraged to call Saddam "Baba" (the Iraqi word for "Daddy"). In school, they were taught that Saddam was a hero, and they were encouraged to tell their teachers if their parents had made any comments about him. Iraqi children soon learned to say nothing, in case a teacher decided their parents should be arrested.

One young boy made a terrible mistake when Saddam himself paid a visit to his school. Saddam took the boy on his knee and asked him if he recognized him. The boy answered, "Yes, of course. Whenever you come on TV, my father spits on the ground and turns it off." After this, the boy and his family were never seen again.[9]

Harsh punishments

During Saddam's rule, people who broke the law faced brutal punishments. Minor thieves often had a hand amputated (cut off), soldiers who deserted the army lost an ear, and armed robbers were executed without trial. Thieves and deserters also had a cross burned onto their forehead, using a red-hot branding iron. The cross was a public sign that they had broken the law.[10]

WAR AND TYRANNY

Within a few months of becoming president, Saddam was preparing for war against Iran, which had a new leader, the Ayatollah Khomeini. In 1979 Iran had experienced a dramatic **Islamic revolution**, in which the Shah (king) was replaced by the Ayatollah Khomeini.[1] The Shah was deeply unpopular among ordinary people, who disliked him for his extravagant lifestyle and blamed him for the Westernization of Iran. This widespread resentment led to a popular uprising and the establishment of an Islamic state led by the Ayatollah, a Shi'a Muslim cleric who was strongly opposed to any Western influences.

Iran hostage crisis

In November 1979, 66 U.S. citizens were held hostage when a group of Islamic students and **militants** took over the U.S. embassy buildings in support of the Iranian Revolution. Despite intensive diplomatic efforts, the Iranian government, led by the Ayatollah, refused to release all of the captives, and 52 Americans remained as hostages until January 1981. The hostage crisis led to widespread hostility in the United States toward the Islamic Republic of Iran. When Ronald Reagan became president in 1981, he increased U.S. support for Saddam against the Iranians.[2]

Under the Ayatollah, Iran's industries were taken over by the state. Strict Muslim laws and schools were introduced, and women and girls had to wear traditional dress and stay at home. The changes in Iran caused widespread concern. Other Arab leaders were afraid that they would face revolution, too. Western leaders feared the spread of an Islamic revolution, which could result in the whole Gulf region turning against the West.

GOING TO WAR

Saddam had several reasons for going to war with Iran. His first motive was to defend his country against the threat of revolution. He feared that the Ayatollah might provoke the

Shi'a majority in Iraq to rise up against him. He was also concerned that Iran might give military support to the Shi'as in Iraq. But Saddam also realized that a war with Iran would provide him with the chance to win valuable land.

In September 1980, Iraqi troops invaded Iran. After attacking airfields around Teheran, they entered the oil-rich region of Khuzestan and claimed it as a **province** of Iraq.[3] This aggressive move broke international law, but Saddam was not prevented from continuing the war. In fact he received secret support from the U.S. government. In the years leading up to the war between Iran and Iraq, the United States had backed the Shah's regime, and the U.S. government was strongly opposed to the Ayatollah, especially after the hostage crisis began in 1979 (see box on page 14).

▷ Ayatollah Khomeini led an Islamic uprising in Iran, which energized all elements of society, like this supporter. The Iranian Revolution caused widespread fear throughout the Arab and Western world.

FOREIGN SUPPORT

In 1982 the United States increased its support of Iraq in the struggle against Iran. It provided Saddam with economic aid, weapons, and military equipment, as well as training for his army.[4] By the end of the war, Saddam was receiving backing from a wide range of countries. The Soviet Union and China, other Arab countries in the Gulf, and a number of European nations all supported Saddam in his attempt to stop the spread of revolutionary Islam. China and the Soviet Union were especially fearful of revolutionary Islam because they had large Muslim populations. Most of this foreign support came in the form of loans and sales of arms (weapons) to Saddam.[5]

KILLING KURDS

Over the course of the Iran-Iraq War, Saddam launched attacks on the Kurds of northern Iraq. Kurdish freedom fighters (belonging to an organization known as Peshmerga) had given their support to the Iranians. Saddam responded with brutal attacks on their villages and towns.

The most violent phase of Saddam's **persecution** of the Kurds was the Anfal campaign, which took place between 1986 and 1989.[6] The leader of this campaign was Ali Hassan al-Majid, known by the Kurds as Chemical Ali because of his use of **chemical weapons**. Following the orders of Chemical Ali, Iraqi troops launched ground attacks and bombing raids on Kurdish communities. Some Kurds were killed by firing squads, while thousands of others were forcibly **deported** (sent away) from their homeland. According to Human Rights Watch (a neutral organization that monitors abuses of human rights), up to 100,000 people were killed in the Anfal campaign. Human Rights Watch also reported that chemical weapons, such as mustard gas and sarin, were being dropped on rebel areas as early as April 1987.[7]

On March 15, 1988, Kurdish freedom fighters captured the town of Halabja, in northern Iraq, from Saddam's forces. They then handed it over to the Iranian army. Even though Halabja was now in Iranian hands, it was still full of innocent Kurdish civilians. But Saddam was ruthless in his revenge. On the following day, he launched a massive chemical attack on Halabja (see pages 18–19). The casualties were enormous: between 3,200 and 5,000 people were killed, and between 7,000 and 10,000 were injured. Many more died in the years after the attack from diseases and birth defects caused by the harmful gases Saddam had used.[8]

BIOGRAPHY

Ali Hassan al-Majid, 1941–2010

BORN: al-Awja, central Iraq

ROLE: Chief of the Iraqi Intelligence Service; defense minister of Iraq

Ali Hassan al-Majid was a Sunni Muslim from a poor family and Saddam Hussein's cousin. After the Ba'ath Party seized power in 1968, he rose very quickly in the Iraqi government, and in 1979 he became chief of the Intelligence Service. Between 1986 and 1989, he led the Anfal campaign. In the 1990s, he was Saddam's defense minister and played a key role in both Gulf wars. Following the invasion of Iraq, he was captured by U.S. troops, tried by an Iraqi court, and sentenced to death by hanging.

Enemy or friend?

Before the Iran-Iraq War, the U.S. government viewed Iraq as a serious threat to the security of the United States. This was because Saddam had formed close friendships with people who were seen as U.S. enemies. In particular, Saddam had given his support to the militant Palestinian Abu Nidal, who was dedicated to opposing U.S. power in the Middle East with violence.

In 1979, the United States had placed Iraq on its list of State Sponsors of Terrorism. However, in 1982 Iraq's name was removed from the list, as the United States began to give its active support to the Iraqis in their war against Iran. This was apparently because Saddam was no longer supporting terrorists. However, this was clearly untrue, since Abu Nidal was based in Baghdad, the capital of Iraq. Later, a U.S. government official admitted: "No one had any doubts about [the Iraqis'] continued involvement in terrorism.... The real reason was to help them succeed in the war in Iran."[9]

EYEWITNESS TO HALABJA

The journalist John Simpson reported from Iraq throughout the period of Saddam's power. He later wrote a book entitled *The Wars Against Saddam: Taking the Hard Road to Baghdad*. Simpson's book contains a vivid description of his experience of visiting Halabja just after the chemical weapons attack on March 16, 1988.[10]

A program of persecution

Saddam's persecution of the Kurds began in the 1970s, when thousands of Kurds were driven out of their traditional homelands. Many escaped into Iran and Turkey, while tens of thousands were forcibly relocated to barren desert sites in southern Iraq. At the same time, Iraqi Arabs were moved into the oil-rich Kurdish regions in a deliberate program of "Arabization." Between 1975 and 1980, around a quarter of a million Kurds were removed from their homes in northern Iraq. This was just the start of an anti-Kurd campaign that reached its peak in the late 1980s.[11]

Simpson was one of a group of Western journalists and photographers invited to visit Halabja in the days following the Iraqi attack. His invitation came from the Iranians, who wanted the world to see the horrors that Iraq had committed. Simpson had heard reports of many thousands of deaths, but he thought that the numbers had been exaggerated. He was in for a terrible shock.

A CITY OF CORPSES

A helicopter dropped him outside Halabja, and he walked toward the town. The first thing he noticed was the stench of rotting bodies. He also saw the corpses of cows and sheep lying in the fields around the town. In Halabja, there were corpses everywhere. People had died suddenly while they were walking down the street or sitting around a table with their families.

Simpson spoke to an old man who witnessed the start of the attack. He described Iraqi planes flying over the town and white smoke coming out of them. The man hid in a concrete shelter for many hours, but when he came out again he saw "a dead place." People he knew were lying dead in the streets or in their houses.

DEADLY GASES

The chemical weapons dumped on Halabja contained a mixture of gases. One of the ingredients was mustard gas, which the Iraqis had already used in battles against the Iranians. Mustard gas causes choking, running eyes and noses, and blistering of the skin. Mixed with the mustard gas was a **nerve gas** called sarin. This prevents the nerves from sending messages to the body's organs, and it causes death by suffocation. Experts also believe that cyanide gas was used at Halabja. Cyanide is a very strong poison that causes instant death, and most of the people of Halabja appeared to have died instantly.

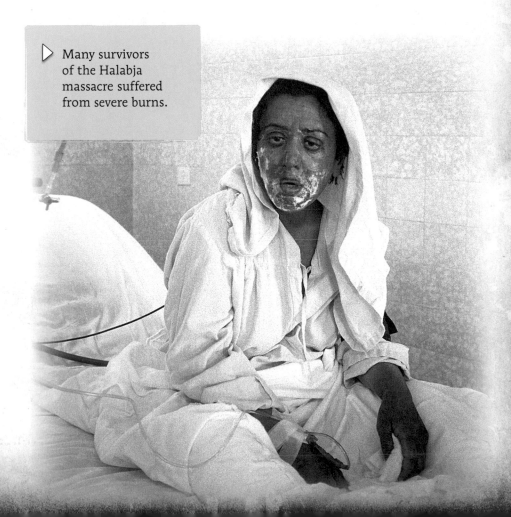

▷ Many survivors of the Halabja massacre suffered from severe burns.

INVADING KUWAIT

The Iran-Iraq War lasted from 1980 to 1988.[1] After eight years of fighting, it ended in a stalemate, with enormous loss of life on both sides but almost no territorial gains. Iraq was drained of its resources, resulting in terrible hardship for the Iraqi people. Saddam was deeply in debt to the nations that had supported him during the war. The Iran-Iraq War had also left another very dangerous legacy. With the help of foreign powers, Saddam had assembled a powerful and well-equipped army, as well as a collection of deadly weapons.

▷ In the late 1980s, the Kuwaitis were greatly envied by the people of Iraq. While Iraq had been crippled by war with Iran, Kuwait had grown steadily richer, thanks to its vast oil reserves.

By the end of the Iran-Iraq War, Iraq was in a desperate situation. An estimated 375,000 Iraqis had died in the war,[2] and the financial costs to Iraq had been huge, totaling more than $400 billion.[3] By 1988, the Iraqi economy had collapsed. The country's oil industry had been badly damaged due to millions of shells landing in Iraqi oil fields over the course of the fighting.

Saddam was in charge of a country with no resources and huge debts. By 1988 he owed an estimated $80 billion to the countries that backed him during the war.[4] The largest portion of this debt was owed to his Arab backers, with around $13 billion due to Kuwait.[5]

TENSIONS WITH KUWAIT

In the period following the Iran-Iraq War, tensions increased between Iraq and neighboring Kuwait. Saddam resented Kuwait's financial success, which had been gained by exploiting its massive oil reserves. In the 1980s, Kuwait had a population of just two million, compared with Iraq's 25 million, but its reserves of oil were roughly the same size as Iraq's.[6]

After the war, Saddam urged the Kuwaitis to show some generosity by canceling his war debt to them. He reminded them that Iraq had fought to defend all Arab countries from the threat of an Islamic revolution. Nevertheless, the Kuwaitis refused to cancel the Iraqi debt. Saddam also suggested that the oil-exporting countries should all cut back on production, in order to raise the world price of oil. He hoped that this measure would help Iraq to pay off its debts more quickly, by giving it greater revenue. However, the Kuwaitis viewed Iraq as a dangerous economic competitor and refused to cooperate in Saddam's plan. Instead, Kuwait overproduced, driving down the price of oil. As Kuwait became steadily richer, Saddam's resentment grew.

Uneasy relations

There had been border disputes between Iraq and Kuwait ever since Britain had negotiated the Kuwait–Saudi border in 1913. In 1961, the Iraqi government claimed Kuwait as its rightful territory.[7] The Iraqis argued that Kuwait had originally been part of the Ottoman province of Basra, and so belonged to Iraq (along with the rest of Basra). They also accused the British of carving the tiny kingdom of Kuwait out of the Ottoman Empire in an attempt to stop other countries from having access to the Persian Gulf. Although the Iraqis failed in their claim, this started a long-running dispute over the Kuwaiti–Iraqi border in Basra province.

By 1990, Saddam was very angry with the Kuwaiti government. He claimed that Kuwait was flooding world markets with low-priced oil in a deliberate move to stop Iraq from recovering from the war. He also complained that the Kuwaitis were practicing "slant drilling" into the Iraqi Rumaila oil field. He claimed the Kuwaitis were sinking diagonal drills into the ground close to the border to steal oil from oil fields under Iraqi territory. However, these complaints were ignored by Kuwait.

TOWARD WAR

Saddam had several reasons for a war against Kuwait. Now that the war in Iran was over, he was left with a large, well-equipped army ready to fight. Saddam was concerned that the returning Iraqi soldiers could turn to violence once they discovered that there were no jobs for them back in Iraq. However, if he used his forces to lead a successful invasion, he would be seen as a powerful leader. Most important of all, conquering Kuwait would bring Saddam enormous wealth, which he could use to solve his country's problems.

Could the United States have stopped Saddam?

Many people have asked why the United States did not try harder to prevent Saddam from invading Kuwait. They have questioned why the **CIA** did not recognize the signs of an approaching invasion. However, it has generally been agreed that no foreign power took Saddam's threats seriously.

In particular, U.S. Ambassador Glaspie has been blamed for not standing up to Saddam. It has even been said that she gave him a "green light" to invade. However, a transcript of their meeting has recently been published on **Wikileaks**, and it makes it clear that Saddam never revealed to her his intention of going to war.[8] At the time, the U.S. government was so confident that there would be no war that Glaspie flew to the United States for a vacation just three days before Saddam's invasion began.

Saddam justified his invasion of Kuwait by claiming that by rights it should belong to Iraq. This was a long-standing claim dating back to the 1960s (see box on page 21). Saddam also declared that the Emir (king) of Kuwait was very unpopular among his subjects. He argued that the Kuwaitis would welcome an invasion, because it would rid them of the Emir and give them more freedom. But this was not entirely true. While the Emir was far from being a democratic ruler, he was generally admired by his people.

By mid-July 1990, Saddam had moved just under 40,000 troops to the Iraq–Kuwait border.[9] This was clearly a threatening move, but other leaders could not be sure whether it was a bluff or a genuine preparation for war. On July 25, April Glaspie, the U.S. **ambassador** in Iraq, held an emergency meeting with Saddam. Glaspie urged Saddam to avoid violence, and Saddam said he would give negotiations one more chance.[10] On July 31, a meeting was held in Jeddah, Saudi Arabia, between the representatives of Iraq and Kuwait, but they failed to reach an agreement.[11] They promised to meet again, but Saddam was already hatching a secret invasion plan.

△ The U.S. ambassador, April Glaspie, has been blamed for failing to stand up to Saddam, but she was simply following her government's policy. In fact, nobody took Saddam's threat of invasion seriously.

WAR

On August 2, 1990, at 2:00 a.m., Iraq launched its attack on Kuwait. Around 100,000 soldiers in armored tanks poured across the border.[12] They advanced south across the desert toward Kuwait City with little resistance, because the Kuwaiti army had not been **mobilized**. The Iraqi ground troops entered the capital, Kuwait City, at around 6:00 a.m.[13] Meanwhile, more troops were arriving by helicopter and boat, and the Iraqi air force was bombing key sites in the city, including the airport.

The Kuwaitis were completely unprepared for the attack. They had no time to mobilize all their forces, although a few units quickly prepared for action and fought back bravely. There was some resistance from troops in army and air force barracks, and one battalion (a unit of around 1,000 soldiers) fought a determined tank battle near Al Jahra, west of Kuwait City. This encounter lasted for several hours before the surviving Kuwaiti troops admitted defeat and escaped to Saudi Arabia.[14]

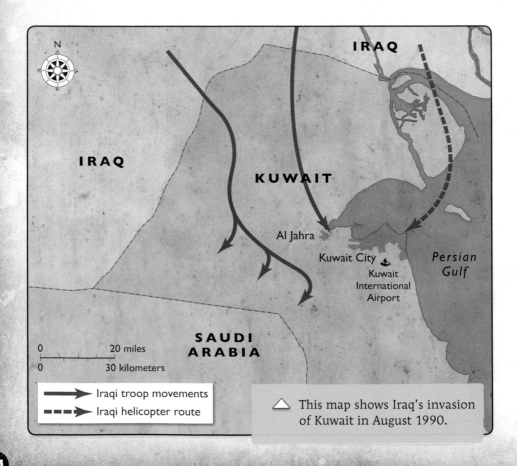

N

IRAQ

IRAQ

KUWAIT

Al Jahra

Kuwait City

Kuwait
International
Airport

*Persian
Gulf*

SAUDI
ARABIA

0   20 miles

0   30 kilometers

→ Iraqi troop movements

----► Iraqi helicopter route

△ This map shows Iraq's invasion of Kuwait in August 1990.

Why were the Kuwaitis unprepared?

The Kuwaiti government made the fatal mistake of failing to recognize just how dangerous Saddam could be. When Iraqi troops began to gather on the border, the Kuwaiti armed forces were put on high alert. But then the Kuwaiti government decided that Saddam's threats of war were not serious. Like the rest of the world, the Kuwaitis did not believe that Saddam would dare to anger his Arab allies by launching an invasion of their country. Instead, they decided that he was simply trying to strengthen his negotiating position. On July 19, the Kuwaiti government gave orders for its troops to stand down.[15] When the surprise invasion came two weeks later, the Kuwaiti troops were not mobilized or ready to fight.

The most important target for the invading Iraqi forces was the Dasman Palace, home of the Emir of Kuwait and his family. The Emir and the crown prince had managed to escape to Saudi Arabia less than an hour before, but the Emir's brother, Prince Fahd, remained inside the palace. Led by Prince Fahd, the Emiri guards put up a brave defense, but Fahd was shot dead on the palace steps, and the Iraqis soon gained control of the palace.[16]

VICTORY FOR SADDAM

By late afternoon on August 2, Iraqi troops were in control of most of Kuwait City. The Kuwaiti army had put up almost no resistance, the navy had never mobilized, and most of the Kuwaiti air force had flown their planes to safety in Saudi Arabia.[17]

Saddam lost no time in taking charge of Kuwait. Within a few days of the invasion, he had claimed Kuwait as the 19th province of Iraq and had installed his cousin, Ali Hassan al-Majid (known as Chemical Ali), as its governor.[18] Some Iraqi units stayed on in Kuwait City, while others headed south toward the border with Saudi Arabia.

INSIDE KUWAIT CITY

For the people of Kuwait City, Saddam's invasion was a terrifying and confusing experience. There were many personal accounts of the dramatic events of August 2, 1990,[19] but one of the best records was provided by the journalist Jenn Cameroon. In an article for the *Arab Times*, she compiled a range of different reactions to the invasion.[20]

INTO A WAR ZONE

Around 6:00 a.m. on the morning of August 2, people were setting off for their usual drive into work. At first, the journey seemed nothing out of the ordinary, but then they were surprised to be caught in a traffic jam on one of the main roads leading into the city. As they checked to find out the cause of the hold-up, they saw a dozen armed Iraqi troops heading toward them.

▽ On the morning of August 2, 1990, the citizens of Kuwait woke up to discover that their streets were filled with Iraqi tanks.

The next minute, they were ordered to get out of their cars and stand on the sidewalk, as the soldiers smashed their windshields with their rifles. They could hear gunfire and explosions. Instead of arriving at work as usual, the Kuwaiti commuters discovered that their peaceful city had become a battleground.[21]

While most Kuwaitis had no idea that invasion was possible, the Emir and his ministers were feeling very worried. The diplomatic meetings in Jeddah had not gone well, and they feared Saddam intended to invade. Nevertheless, it still came as a terrible shock when they were informed soon after 2:00 a.m. that Saddam's forces had crossed the Kuwaiti border. Desperate orders were given for the Kuwaiti forces to prepare for action, but it was much too late. By 4:00 a.m. the rumble of approaching tanks could be heard in Kuwait City. At 4:35 a.m. the crown prince succeeded in persuading his father, the Emir of Kuwait, that their only option was escape. They rushed to the U.S. embassy, where they were airlifted out of the city by helicopter. Less than half an hour afterward, Iraqi soldiers started firing at the palace.[22]

Capture at the airport

Passengers on British Airways flight 149 to Kuala Lumpur via Kuwait City had no idea they were flying into a war zone. When they left London at around 7:00 p.m., their pilot was informed that there wasn't any trouble in Kuwait. However, by 4:00 a.m., when their plane landed at Kuwait City airport, Saddam's troops had already reached the city. Some passengers entered the airport, not realizing that they were now trapped inside Kuwait. Others waited in the plane, wondering why it did not take off again.

Within an hour, the passengers and crew had all been captured by Iraqi troops. One passenger—a member of the Kuwaiti royal family—was killed by the Iraqis, while most of the other passengers were held as hostages. Some of the hostages were kept as prisoners in Kuwait and Iraq for up to five months. During that period, some of them were imprisoned in horrible conditions.[23]

FIRST GULF WAR

The invasion of Kuwait took the world completely by surprise. Everyone had believed that Iraq's disagreements with Kuwait could be resolved through peaceful means, but now Iraqi tanks occupied Kuwait City. Within hours of the invasion, the **United Nations (UN)** Security Council met to discuss the situation. The UN Security Council is responsible for international peace and security. It is made up of representatives from many nations, who can each put forward their point of view before a vote is taken and a decision made to pass a **resolution**. On August 2, the council issued a resolution condemning the invasion and demanding that Iraqi troops should withdraw from Kuwait.[1]

A DANGEROUS THREAT

Saddam's invasion posed a serious economic threat to foreign powers. Now that Kuwait was conquered, Saddam controlled 20 percent of the world's oil supplies. His armies were also gathered along the border of Saudi Arabia, preparing to invade. If Iraq went on to defeat the Saudis, Saddam would gain control of 40 percent of the world's total oil reserves.[2]

Faced with this dangerous situation, the U.S. government decided that its first move should be to defend Saudi Arabia from attack. President George H. W. Bush negotiated with the Saudi ruler, King Fahd, to allow U.S. troops to be based in his country.

King Fahd had to make a difficult decision. His first priority was to protect his country from invasion. But Saudi Arabia was a highly conservative Muslim nation and the home of Mecca, the holiest place in the Islamic world. If Fahd said yes to President Bush, it would mean allowing thousands of Christian soldiers into his country. However, the Saudis were in obvious need of military support. Despite their well-trained army and modern weaponry, their forces were nowhere near as large as the Iraqi military. The Saudi army also had close links with the U.S. and UK militaries. Many of its officers had trained with U.S. or UK forces and used equipment made in the United States or the United Kingdom.

Eventually, King Fahd agreed to the U.S. plan, which was code named Operation Desert Shield.

On August 6, 1990, plans were put in motion to move a quarter of a million troops into Saudi Arabia.[3] Over the next few weeks, the United States also sent fighter jets, tanks, battleships, and aircraft carriers. Around-the-clock flying patrols were soon established on the Saudi borders, to keep a constant lookout for any Iraqi military advances. Operation Desert Shield had begun.

George H. W. Bush

BORN: Milton, Massachussetts, 1924

ROLE: President of the United States, 1989–1993

Bush was educated at a private school and joined the U.S. Navy at the age of 18. He served as a pilot in the navy during World War II (1939–45). After the war, Bush studied economics at Yale University, before joining an oil company in Texas. He became a **Republican** senator in 1966, and 10 years later he was appointed director of the CIA. In 1980, Bush became Ronald Reagan's vice president, and in 1988 he was elected president. Bush led the Coalition in the First Gulf War and made the decision to end the war directly after the Iraqis had been driven out of Kuwait. In 1992, he lost the presidential election to **Democrat** Bill Clinton.[4]

DIPLOMATIC PRESSURE

While the United States was setting up Operation Desert Shield, the UN Security Council continued to put pressure on Iraq. On August 6, UN Resolution 661 placed international **trade sanctions** on Iraq.[5] These sanctions banned any trade between Iraq or Kuwait and the rest of the world, with the aim of frightening Saddam into withdrawing his troops. The UN later added another resolution, allowing a **naval blockade** to be established in the Persian Gulf. Ships in this blockade were authorized to stop all shipping, in order to make sure that the trade sanctions were obeyed.

The sanctions imposed by the UN had the unfortunate result of making life much harder for the Iraqi people, but they did nothing to change Saddam's mind. As the months went past, it became clear that Saddam did not intend to withdraw from Kuwait.

▽ Between August and November 1990, the United Nations imposed a series of sanctions on Iraq, but none of them achieved the result of forcing Saddam to withdraw his troops.

Iraq's weapons of mass destruction

Weapons of mass destruction (WMDs) can be chemical (usually taking the form of poisonous gases or sprays), **biological** (gases, powders, or sprays containing germs that cause deadly diseases), or **nuclear** (either in the form of a nuclear bomb or a nuclear **missile**). These WMDs can kill people in very large numbers, and in the 1980s there was evidence that Saddam was developing all three types.

During the Iran-Iraq War, Saddam's army used a range of chemical weapons, such as the gases dumped on Halabja (see pages 16–19). Iraqi scientists were known to be working on biological weapons.[6] There were also signs that Saddam might be developing a nuclear bomb, as the Iraqis had several **nuclear reactors**.[7] The question of whether Saddam still had any WMDs in 2003 was a major issue in the events leading up to the Second Gulf War (see pages 46–49).

Eventually, the UN decided it was time for action, and in November 1990 it passed Resolution 678. This gave Iraq until January 15, 1991, to withdraw from Kuwait. It also allowed the use of "all necessary means" to force Iraq out of Kuwait after the deadline.[8]

JUSTIFYING THE WAR

As part of its preparations for war, the U.S. government produced a list of reasons for fighting Saddam. First and foremost, it claimed that Iraq had broken international law by invading Kuwait. It also highlighted Saddam's record of **human rights abuses**, in his cruel treatment of Iraqi citizens.

U.S.-government spokespeople also stressed the threat posed to the world by Iraq's stock of deadly weapons. During the 1980s, Saddam had developed some dangerous **weapons of mass destruction (WMDs)**. By waging war on Saddam, the United States aimed to destroy these weapons and prevent Saddam from producing any more. The justifications for war were presented publicly by the U.S. government.

BUILDING A COALITION

As the UN deadline approached, the U.S. government worked hard
to assemble a coalition of nations that would help to drive the Iraqis
out of Kuwait. Not all nations were convinced that it was right
for Western powers to intervene in the politics of the Middle East.
Eventually, a total of 34 countries joined the Coalition.[9] Almost
75 percent of the military forces were American, while Saudi Arabia,
the United Kingdom, Egypt, and Syria each made a major contribution
in terms of manpower and equipment. Some countries, such as
Germany and Japan, had laws preventing their soldiers from being
used overseas, but they provided financial aid instead.

By January 1991 it was clear that Saddam was going to ignore the
UN deadline. The Coalition prepared to take action, and one day after
the deadline had lapsed, it launched an extensive bombing campaign
over Kuwait and Iraq.[10] This aerial warfare also included cruise
missiles launched from U.S. warships in the Persian Gulf.

The main aim of the Coalition bombers was to destroy Iraqi air
force bases and anti-aircraft equipment. They also targeted military
command centers, missile launchers, weapons research units, and
naval bases. Coalition aircraft met surprisingly little opposition from
the Iraqis. Over the course of the First Gulf War, the Coalition made

▽ Before the war started, Iraqi Scud missiles were greatly feared,
because it was believed that they would hold chemical weapons.
In fact, they did not carry WMDs, and very few hit their targets.

a total of 100,000 flights, but lost only 75 planes, of which just 44 were shot down by Iraqi planes and ground fire.[11] The Iraqi air force was powerless against such vast Coalition numbers, and some Iraqi pilots flew to Iran and surrendered there.

Within a month the Coalition forces had gained total superiority in the air. This meant that the Coalition could pinpoint all the Iraqi forces, while the Iraqis could not carry out any air observations.

As soon as the bombing raids began, the Iraqis responded by launching their **Scud missiles**. These are long-range weapons that can travel overland for hundreds of miles and cause serious damage.

DRAWING IN ISRAEL

Some of Saddam's missiles were directed at the Coalition forces in Saudi Arabia. Others were launched at Israel, with the aim of drawing the Israelis into the conflict. Saddam hoped that his attacks would provoke Israel into joining the Coalition against Iraq. If this happened, Saddam was confident that the Arab nations in the Coalition would withdraw, rather than fight alongside the Israelis, their long-term enemies in the wider Middle East conflict.

It was a clever plan, but it did not succeed. The Israelis followed the advice of the United States and did not respond to the Scud attacks, so all the Arab nations stayed in the Coalition. President Bush persuaded Israel by promising to protect Israeli cities. Coalition troops used surface-to-air missiles (known as Patriot missiles) to shoot down some of the Scuds. Special-forces soldiers from the United States and United Kingdom also conducted Scud hunts, searching for secret launching pads hidden in the deserts of Kuwait and Iraq.

Bravo Two Zero

In 1991 an eight-man British **SAS** unit was given the task of hunting for Scud missile launchers in the Iraqi desert. Over the course of its mission, the unit had some terrifying encounters, and not all of the soldiers survived. One of the soldiers described his experiences in a book, which he called *Bravo Two Zero*, after his unit's **call sign**.[12] *Bravo Two Zero* tells an exciting story, but it was later shown that it is not entirely accurate.

A HIGH-TECH WAR

The First Gulf War introduced a new kind of hi-tech warfare. It has been called "the first space war" because of the Coalition forces' use of satellite communications and other space-age technology.

Coalition "stealth" bombers are shown ready for action. The Coalition used its state-of-the art military technology to wage a remarkably effective air campaign.

The Coalition forces had a remarkable range of state-of-the-art equipment. Modern fighter-bomber planes carried **smart bombs** (also known as precision guided missiles), which could hit their targets with pinpoint accuracy. "Stealth" bombers, such as the Lockheed F-117 Nighthawk, were designed to fly almost silently and avoid detection on radar screens. Surface-to-air missiles could find and destroy planes or other missiles in mid-air.

Coalition forces also benefited from **satellite technology**. Army commanders used satellites to help them navigate through the desert and to track the movements of enemy troops. Soldiers used early versions of cell phones to communicate with each other, and satellite technology was used to observe changes in weather conditions.

The Coalition commanders were eager to demonstrate to the public that they were doing as much as possible to avoid civilian casualties. By using smart bombs, which could be aimed directly at military targets, they claimed that they could prevent the deaths of innocent victims. However, civilian casualties could not be entirely avoided.

On February 13, 1991, two smart bombs were dropped on what was wrongly believed to be an Iraqi military control center in the Amiriyah neighborhood of Baghdad. The bombs hit an air-raid shelter, killing more than 400 Iraqi civilians.[13]

Saddam also had some impressive military equipment. His army (which totaled roughly a million men) had nearly 6,000 armored tanks and around 200 helicopters.[14] The Iraqi air force had more than 900 planes, carrying a range of missiles, including some smart bombs.[15] In addition, Iraq possessed surface-to-air missiles and powerful Scud missiles.

Despite Saddam's apparent strengths, his forces were not as disciplined as the Coalition troops. His generals lacked a clear strategy, and the Iraqis' weapons and equipment, which were mainly supplied by the Soviet Union, were old-fashioned and much less effective than those of the Coalition.

WATCHING THE WAR

The First Gulf War could be watched on television almost as it happened. Some war reporters and camera crews were "embedded" in army units, living alongside the soldiers of the Coalition as they were fighting the war. The reporters' live broadcasts provided people all over the world with a vivid sense of the horror and drama of war. Military leaders gave frequent briefings to the press to keep the public informed of events. These briefings included pictures taken during combat, to show the world the effectiveness of the Coalition attacks.

Scud attacks

Over the course of the First Gulf War, Iraq fired a total of 91 Scud missiles. Of these, just over 50 percent were aimed at Saudi Arabia, and around three at Bahrain, while the remainder were fired into Israel. In Israel, only two people died as a direct consequence of the strikes, while just over 200 were injured, only one of them seriously. The most extensive damage was caused by a missile that landed on a U.S. Army barracks in Saudi Arabia, killing 28 soldiers and injuring just under 100.[16]

VICTORY AT A COST

After four weeks of bombing raids, the Coalition moved on to the next phase—war on the ground. The land campaign proved to be the shortest part of the war, even though the Coalition commanders had expected it to be the riskiest phase. In the air, the Coalition had gained complete superiority. But on the ground, the two sides appeared to be much more evenly matched.

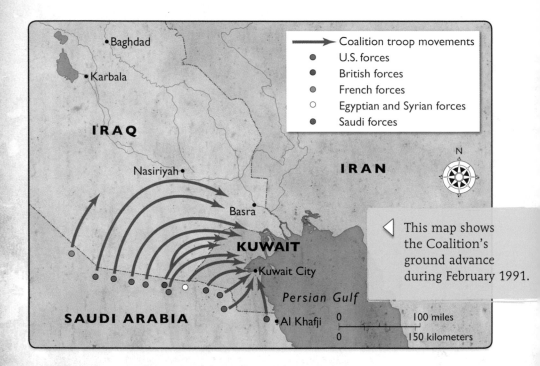

• Baghdad

• Karbala

IRAQ

Nasiriyah•

Basra•

KUWAIT

•Kuwait City

Persian Gulf

SAUDI ARABIA   •Al Khafji

IRAN

N

→ Coalition troop movements
- U.S. forces
- British forces
- French forces
- ○ Egyptian and Syrian forces
- Saudi forces

0   100 miles

0   150 kilometers

This map shows the Coalition's ground advance during February 1991.

THE BATTLE OF AL KHAFJI

The first challenge for the Coalition ground force occurred even before its campaign had begun. On January 29, 1991, Saddam's army launched an attack on the Saudi city of Al Khafji, near the border with Kuwait.[1] The Coalition was caught by surprise, and Iraqi troops soon occupied the city. However, the Coalition fought back, and after two days of heavy fighting, the Iraqis were driven out of Al Khafji. For the Iraqis, the battle was a disaster. Only 20 percent of their attacking force managed to make it back into Iraqi territory.[2]

The Coalition ground campaign, code named Operation Desert Sabre, began at 4:00 a.m. on February 24, 1991.[3] The U.S. commander of armed forces, General Norman Schwarzkopf, had planned the campaign very carefully. While some divisions marched directly north toward Kuwait City, others took a less direct approach—first heading north and then turning east (see map). This army maneuver (move) has been compared to a "left hook"—a surprise move used by boxers.

BIOGRAPHY

General Norman Schwarzkopf

BORN: Trenton, New Jersey, 1934

ROLE: Commander-in-chief of Coalition forces in the First Gulf War

Norman Schwarzkopf trained as an army officer at the United States Military Academy, West Point, and has a master's degree in missile engineering. As a young officer, he served in the Vietnam War (1955–75), where he was awarded a Silver Star for rescuing a wounded man and leading a group of soldiers through a minefield to safety. He was later awarded two more Silver Stars for bravery in war. In 1988, Schwarzkopf was appointed commander-in-chief of the U.S. Central Command, and the following year he was put in charge of Operation Desert Sabre. His strategy for the ground assault was widely credited with bringing the final stage of the First Gulf War to a close in just four days. During the last stages of the war, Schwarzkopf gave almost daily press conferences to report on the progress of his campaign.[4]

ADVANCING TO VICTORY

The Coalition army had expected to meet fierce opposition on the ground, but it soon discovered that the Iraqi military had been devastated by the air attacks. Cut off from their supply bases, thousands of Iraqi soldiers simply surrendered, and the advancing Coalition troops spent most of their time taking prisoners rather than fighting.[5] In a few places, the better-trained forces, such as Saddam's Republican Guard, put up a determined fight, but their outdated equipment proved no match for the Coalition weapons. The U.S. and UK tank guns could shoot farther and their tanks had better armor than the Iraqi vehicles. The Coalition could also fight at night, while its helicopter support included tank-busting AH-64 Apaches.

Even in Kuwait City, Coalition forces met very little armed resistance. As they reached the city's outskirts, Saddam's troops poured out of the capital, and by the evening of February 26 the Coalition had taken control of Kuwait City.[6]

As Iraqi troops retreated back into Iraq, they came under heavy tank fire and air attacks. The six-lane highway running northwest from Kuwait City to Iraq was littered with burned-out vehicles and charred corpses, earning it the name "Highway of Death."

Did the Coalition stop too soon?

Some people criticized the Coalition commanders for stopping the war too soon. Critics said that Coalition forces should have continued into Iraq and **deposed** Saddam. However, President Bush defended his actions strongly. In a book published in 1998, he argued that such a move would have split the Coalition, because its Arab allies would have strongly opposed any takeover of Iraq by the United States. While there was international agreement or support for the expulsion of Saddam from Kuwait, no agreement had been made on how to run Iraq if Saddam were overthrown. Bush also predicted that any attempt to seize power in Iraq would have resulted in enormous loss of life.[7] Rather than depose Saddam themselves, Bush's government hoped that Saddam would be overthrown by a rebellion within Iraq. But Saddam proved too powerful for any rebels to challenge him.

The scenes of devastation on the Highway of Death appeared on television screens around the world. The Coalition leaders realized that such horrific images could easily turn public opinion against their actions. They recognized the fact that while many people supported a war to remove the Iraqis from Kuwait, most would not support an invasion of Iraq. It was clearly time to consider calling a halt to the war.

In an act of defiance, retreating Iraqi troops set fire to around 700 Kuwaiti oil wells. They also planted **land mines** around the wells to make the fires very difficult to put out. It was 10 months before all the fires could be extinguished. During that time, around 6 million barrels of oil were lost each day.[8] The fires also caused widespread pollution in the Gulf region.

CEASE-FIRE

At 8:00 a.m. on February 28, President Bush ordered a cease-fire.[9] For the next few days, there were scattered outbreaks of violence, but on March 3, 1991, Iraq accepted the terms of the cease-fire.[10] These terms required Iraq to end all military action, to give up Kuwait, to reveal information about any stored chemical and biological weapons, to release all international prisoners, and to accept responsibility for the casualties and damage done during its occupation of Kuwait. The First Gulf War had come to an end.

◁ Teams of firefighters worked for months to cap over 700 burning wells in the Kuwaiti desert. The famous Texan firefighter Red Adair played a key role in coordinating the campaign.

DESERT WARFARE

While the Coalition was launching its air attacks, the troops on the ground were waiting nervously for their part in the war to begin. They were stationed in the Saudi desert, which was a very bleak place to be in early January. After the searing heat of the summer months, a desert winter had set in. The temperature had dropped to almost zero, a constant rain turned the desert sand to sticky mud, and the wind lashed cruelly against the soldiers' faces, which were chapped and raw from exposure to the extreme desert weather.

Apart from their concerns about the approaching conflict, Coalition troops also had to cope with the prospect of a chemical or biological attack. Soldiers were given shots to protect them against anthrax and other poisons. They were given masks and protective suits, and they carried out safety drills to prepare themselves for attacks from weapons of mass destruction. All of these preparations added to the sense of anxiety and tension among the troops.

All the troops had been prepared to meet a very dangerous opponent. One of their commanders warned that the campaign would not be "a walk in the woods," and went on to say: "These boys [the Iraqis] have the fourth-largest army in the world. They're not going to just roll over. I fully expect we will have 10 percent casualties in the first week.... You're going to have to prepare yourself for that."[11]

When the fighting finally began, Coalition troops were astonished to discover just how weak the Iraqi forces were. Much of Saddam's army was made up of conscripts (people who had been forced to fight). One U.S. soldier described his surprise as he prepared to fight a group of highly trained professional soldiers, only to discover that they were all young boys or old men: "They were a sad sight, with absolutely no fight left in them. What weapons they had were in bad repair and little **ammunition** was on hand. They were hungry, cold, and scared.... These people had no business being on a battlefield."[12]

At every stage of the ground campaign, the Coalition discovered that its equipment, training, and discipline were far superior to those of its opponents. As one U.S. soldier said, "The folks we fought never had a chance."[13]

⚠ Wrecked Iraqi vehicles are left on the Highway of Death in February 1991. The Coalition commanders have been criticized for their heavy bombardment of Saddam's retreating troops.

Gulf War syndrome

Some of the Coalition soldiers who fought in the First Gulf War suffered long-term effects. They developed a range of physical problems, including extreme fatigue (tiredness), dizziness, joint and muscle pain, stomach complaints, and skin problems. This set of symptoms has been given the name Gulf War syndrome. Around 25 percent of all U.S. Gulf War veterans (ex-soldiers) appear to suffer to some degree from Gulf War syndrome.[14] In many cases, their symptoms are so severe that they are unable to work.

Medical experts disagree about the causes of Gulf War syndrome, while some even question whether it is a real illness at all. Soldiers may have become ill because they were exposed to ammunition (such as tank shells) made using a dense metal called depleted uranium, which can pierce armor. They may have reacted badly to the many shots that they were given to protect them against chemical weapons and infectious diseases. Or they may have been affected by the strong chemicals in the insect-repellent sprays that were used in the desert.

AN UNEASY PEACE

After the First Gulf War, the UN insisted that Saddam must destroy all his chemical and biological weapons. Saddam had to agree to regular visits from UN weapons inspectors, who would make sure that the Iraqis were not producing any more WMDs. The UN also continued to impose trade sanctions on Iraq, although it did express concern about the desperate situation of the Iraqi people. These sanctions, which had first been imposed when Saddam invaded Kuwait, banned other countries from trading goods with Iraq and also prevented Iraq from exporting its oil, except in payment for its debts.

In the years following the invasion of Kuwait, Saddam's methods of government became even more brutal than before. At the same time, Saddam's two sons, Uday and Qusay, each conducted their own reigns of terror (see box). The people of Iraq lived in a state of constant fear. They also suffered greatly because of their country's economic problems. After two wars, Iraq's economy was in a desperate state, while the UN sanctions made recovery impossible.

Uday and Qusay Hussein

Uday Hussein was born in 1964 and was the oldest of Saddam's two sons. He ran several newspapers and television and radio stations and was in charge of the Iraqi soccer team. He was widely feared for his violence, which included torturing the soccer players he trained. He was also notorious for his incredibly extravagant lifestyle.[1]

Qusay Hussein was born in 1966. In 2000 he was appointed as his father's successor, after Uday was badly injured in an assassination attempt. Qusay played a central role in crushing the Shi'a uprising after the First Gulf War. He also executed thousands of political prisoners, in order to make more room in Iraq's crowded jails.[2] After the Coalition invasion of Iraq in 2003, Uday and Qusay went into hiding. They were surrounded and killed by U.S. troops on July 22, 2003.[3] At the time of their deaths, Uday was 39 and Qusay was 37.

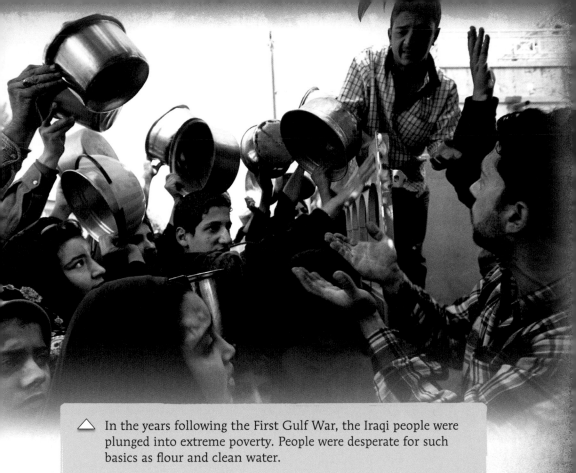

△ In the years following the First Gulf War, the Iraqi people were plunged into extreme poverty. People were desperate for such basics as flour and clean water.

TERRIBLE CONDITIONS

By the late 1990s in Iraq, 25 percent of children under the age of five were suffering from malnutrition, the rate of infant deaths had risen to among the highest in the world, and less than 50 percent of the Iraqi population had access to clean water.[4] The price of food rocketed, and people were forced to eat whatever they could find. Families survived on flour made from a mixture of date seeds, corncobs, and wood shavings. Meanwhile, Saddam was building luxurious palaces for himself and his family and reequipping the Iraqi army.

In December 1996 the UN introduced an "Oil for Food" program, in an attempt to ease the problems in Iraq.[5] The program allowed Saddam's government to sell limited amounts of oil in return for food and medicine, but it could not solve such a serious situation.

NO-FLY ZONES

After the fighting of the First Gulf War was over, some Coalition troops stayed on in Saudi Arabia. They feared that Saddam might try to attack the Saudis, and their suspicions were proven when Saddam launched bombing raids on rebel Shi'a Muslims in southern Iraq. Saddam's bombs were worryingly close to the Saudi border and prompted the Coalition to take defensive action. It set up Operation Southern Watch, establishing strict **no-fly zones** over southern Iraq. These zones were mainly policed by U.S. troops and pilots operating anti-aircraft missiles and planes.

Between 1992 and 1996, there were many minor clashes as Iraqi planes entered the no-fly zone and were shot down. Most of these events went unreported, but some major attacks were featured in the press. In 1993 U.S. troops in Saudi Arabia launched a missile attack on Iraq's intelligence headquarters in Baghdad.[6] This strike followed claims that Saddam had plotted to assassinate President Bush while he was in Kuwait. When Iraqi forces invaded the Kurdish regions of northern Iraq in 1996, U.S. forces responded at once, launching Operation Desert Strike, aimed at military targets in north and south Iraq.[7]

In 1998 U.S. President Bill Clinton authorized the largest strike so far. Operation Desert Fox was a three-day air campaign waged against military targets all over Iraq.[8] Clinton said that Operation Desert Fox was a direct punishment for Saddam. He had broken UN sanctions by smuggling goods into Iraq. But much more important than this, he had refused to cooperate with UN weapons inspectors.

WEAPONS INSPECTIONS

Between 1992 and 1997, inspectors from **UNSCOM** (the United Nations organization responsible for checking for WMDs in Iraq) made regular visits to Iraq.[9] However, by the late 1990s Saddam had begun to voice strong objections to the inspections. He claimed that members of the team were passing on military information to the U.S. government—a claim that was later revealed to be correct.[10] On December 16, 1998, UNSCOM chief Richard Butler reported that the Iraqis were refusing to cooperate with his team.[11] Just a few hours later, Clinton launched Operation Desert Fox.

△ A UN weapons inspection team arrives in Iraq. Most of the inspectors were American, and Saddam objected that they were acting as military spies for the U.S. government.

"Too near to Mecca"

Many Muslims were upset and angry when Coalition troops remained in Saudi Arabia after the First Gulf War. Muslims found it especially upsetting that U.S. troops were so close to the city of Mecca, believed to be the birthplace of the Prophet Muhammad and a place of pilgrimage for Muslims everywhere. During the 1990s, Osama bin Laden, who later masterminded the 9/11 terrorist attack on New York City and Washington, D.C., made many protests against the presence of U.S. troops in Saudi Arabia. In 1999, he stated in an interview that the Americans were too near to Mecca, a position he saw as a provocation to the entire Muslim world.[12] After 9/11, bin Laden claimed that the presence of U.S. troops in Islamic holy places was one of the reasons for his attack on the United States.[13]

NEGOTIATIONS AND SUSPICIONS

In 1999 UNSCOM was replaced with a new organization, UNMOVIC (UN Monitoring, Verification, and Inspection Commission), and in the following year Hans Blix was appointed as its chairman.[14] Blix came from Sweden, a country that is officially neutral and not a part of any political or military alliance, so Saddam could not claim that he was an enemy of Iraq. In August 2002, Saddam allowed Blix to enter Iraq for "technical talks."[15]

This was a positive step, but it did not stop the suspicions about Saddam that were growing in the United States and the United Kingdom. The U.S. and UK leaders—President George W. Bush (the son of George H. W. Bush, who was president during the First Gulf War) and Prime Minister Tony Blair—were both convinced that Saddam was developing WMDs. In July 2002, the ex-chief weapons inspector, Richard Butler, told a U.S. Senate committee that Iraq had stepped up its production of chemical and biological weapons after 1998.[16] He also warned that Saddam might be close to developing a nuclear bomb. In September the UK government published a document appearing to show that Saddam was developing WMDs (see pages 48–49). Adding to this suspicion, some of Saddam's speeches seemed to suggest he had the ability to strike at Western forces, giving the impression that he still had some WMDs.

In an atmosphere of growing suspicion, the U.S. government repeatedly threatened military action if Saddam refused to allow weapons inspections. This relentless pressure finally achieved some results in November 2002, when Saddam reluctantly agreed to allow Blix and his inspection team to enter Iraq.[17] Blix personally warned Saddam against playing "cat and mouse" games with his team and warned Iraq of "serious consequences" if it attempted to delay his mission.

HANS BLIX REPORTS

In February 2003, Hans Blix reported that, so far, his team had found no clear and complete evidence for the production of WMDs.[18] Blix's inspection work continued against a background of U.S. preparations for war, and by March it was clear that President Bush intended to strike against Iraq very soon.

In early March, Blix reported that there was still no clear evidence of WMDs, but he also said that he needed more time to finish his work.

He estimated that a complete inspection process "would not take years, nor weeks, but months."[19] In spite of this report, President Bush went ahead with his invasion plans.

RUMSFELD AND CHENEY

Two key members of President Bush's administration played an active part in pushing the United States toward war. Donald Rumsfeld was secretary of defense from 2001 to 2006.[20] He insisted that a war with Iraq would be over very quickly. Speaking in February 2003, he said, "It could last six days, six weeks. I doubt six months."[21] Dick Cheney was Bush's vice president and had also been secretary of defense for President George H. W. Bush, directing operations in the First Gulf War. From 1995 until 2000, Cheney was chairman of the company Halliburton,[22] which sold services and technology to oil and gas companies. Many people believed that his passion for war with Saddam was strongly motivated by his commercial interest in gaining control of Iraqi oil reserves. In the months leading up to the war, Cheney made public claims that there was a connection between Saddam Hussein and **al-Qaeda**, even though he had seen a CIA report stating there was no evidence for such a link.[23]

"War on terror"

By 2002 President Bush was leading a passionate campaign against Iraq. He claimed that Iraq belonged to a group of countries, which he called the "axis of evil," that were all sworn enemies of the United States.[24] Bush's campaign against the axis of evil was prompted by the terrorist attack on the United States that took place on September 11, 2001, when two planes were hijacked and flown into the World Trade Center's twin towers in New York City. The attack was the work of the Muslim terrorist organization al-Qaeda, and Bush's first response was to launch a "war on terror" in October 2001, by fighting the forces of al-Qaeda in Afghanistan.[25] The initial phase of this war in Afghanistan was a partial success for the United States, but Americans still felt under threat from hostile Muslim countries. By 2002 Bush was eager to extend his war on terror to Iraq. One of the reasons he gave was that al-Qaeda had bases in Iraq. However, no solid evidence was ever found for this claim.

ANY EVIDENCE?

As the United States and United Kingdom prepared for war, Bush and Blair both made claims that Saddam was developing chemical, biological, and even nuclear weapons. However, most of their claims about WMDs have since been proven to be untrue.

Bush and Blair both made very precise claims about Saddam's WMDs. Bush said that Saddam was six months away from developing a nuclear weapon.[26] He also said that yellowcake uranium, an essential ingredient in making nuclear weapons, was being smuggled into Iraq from Africa.[27] Blair was even more specific, saying that Saddam's WMDs could be activated in 45 minutes.[28] Many of the claims were based on two UK-government documents, known as the September Dossier and the February Dossier. Both were later shown to contain inaccurate and unproven information. The press nicknamed the February Dossier the "dodgy dossier," meaning it was unreliable.

BRAVE PROTESTERS

Some courageous individuals dared to insist that their governments were presenting false evidence. In the United States, Joseph Wilson (an ex-ambassador to Africa) was sent by the CIA to Africa to confirm that Saddam was buying yellowcake uranium. Wilson found no evidence of sales to Iraq, and in July 2003 he went on national television to deny the government's claims. As a result of Wilson's actions, his wife, Valerie Plame, was instantly dismissed from her job as a secret CIA agent. More worryingly, Plame's name and role were leaked to the press. Because Plame had worked as an undercover agent on some very dangerous missions, there were many people who wanted her dead, and she was suddenly in great personal danger.

The case of Wilson and Plame was examined in a court of law, and several members of Bush's government were found guilty of leaking information about Plame's secret role in the CIA. One of them— Lewis ("Scooter") Libby—was sentenced to 30 months in jail, but President Bush reduced the term.

In 2002 Dr. David Kelly, a UK expert on weapons technology, spoke to a journalist about his concerns over some information in the UK government's September Dossier. Acting on this information,

△ The story of Joseph Wilson and his wife, Valerie Plame, has been made into an exciting movie called *Fair Game*.

the journalist, Andrew Gilligan, published the claim that the September Dossier had been altered and exaggerated by the UK government to make a stronger case against Saddam. Blair's government was furious, and Kelly was summoned to meet a group of government officials who wanted to investigate his claims. Kelly was so distressed by the situation that he committed suicide in July 2003.

Following the Coalition invasion of Iraq in 2003, the Iraq Survey Group was formed. Its task was to search Iraq for WMDs or factories making WMDs. In October 2003, the group issued its final report, known as the Duelfer Report.[29] It stated that no significant WMDs had been found, and that the team had not discovered any workable WMD programs. The findings of the report contradicted most of the claims presented by Bush and Blair before they went to war.

Embarrassing facts

In February 2011, an Iraqi man code named Curveball admitted that he had supplied false evidence of WMDs to the CIA in the period leading up to the Iraq War. It was also revealed that the CIA had been warned that Curveball's evidence—he claimed to have been an engineer who had worked on biological weapons laboratories—could not be trusted.[30]

SECOND GULF WAR

By early 2003, President George W. Bush and his government were preparing for war with Iraq. Their aims were to find and destroy all WMDs and remove Saddam from power. However, before the United States could invade Iraq, it had to persuade the UN to agree to the war. It also had to find allies to form a "coalition of the willing."

PERSUADING THE UN

Bush's closest ally in his campaign against Saddam was the UK prime minister, Tony Blair. He also had support from the Spanish prime minister, José María Aznar. These three leaders proposed that the UN should threaten Saddam with military action if he did not agree to destroy all his illegal weapons. However, this proposal was rejected by other UN members. In particular, France, Germany, Canada, and Russia were opposed to military action in Iraq.

On February 5, 2003, the U.S. secretary of state, Colin Powell, appeared before the UN to present evidence that Iraq was producing WMDs.[1] Powell stated that he had no doubt Saddam was preparing to make nuclear weapons. Powell was admired as a fine military general and a moderate politician. His speech helped to persuade other countries to join a coalition with the United States.

Bush and Blair gave several reasons for going to war. First, they claimed that Saddam had WMDs that he planned to use against Western powers. Second, they pointed to Saddam's record of human rights abuses. They also accused Saddam of supporting al-Qaeda agents, although no evidence for this was ever found. Another reason given for invasion was Iraq's support of Palestinian terrorists.

OPPOSING THE WAR

Not all countries were convinced by the arguments for war. In the early months of 2003, the French government led the international opposition. Opponents questioned the evidence for the existence of Iraqi WMDs and warned that a war with Iraq would threaten world security. They urged that pressure should be put on Saddam by diplomatic means, rather than by waging war. On February 4, 2003,

the French president, Jacques Chirac, held a meeting with Tony Blair, in which he declared that "war is the worst option" and called for UN weapons inspectors to be allowed to continue their work.[2] In the months leading up to the war, Chirac faced criticism from the United States and the United Kingdom. However, his views on the consequences of the war have proved to be remarkably accurate.

BIOGRAPHY

George W. Bush

BORN: New Haven, Connecticut, 1946

ROLE: President of the United States, 2001–2009

George W. Bush is the eldest son of President George H. W. Bush. In 1994 he was elected governor of Texas, representing the Republican Party. In 2000 he ran against the Democrat candidate, Al Gore, in the U.S. presidential election. Bush won the election, but he failed to gain the majority of votes. Eight months after Bush was elected, he announced a "war on terror" in response to the 9/11 attacks. In 2001 he led the United States into war in Afghanistan. Two years later, he launched the Second Gulf War. In 2009 Bush was succeeded as president by Democrat Barack Obama.[3]

⚠ Antiwar protestors marched through London, England, on February 16, 2003. They were part of a worldwide protest against Bush and Blair's plans to invade Iraq.

PUBLIC PROTESTS

As war in Iraq became more likely, public protests against it were held in cities around the world. On the weekend of February 15–16, between 6 and 10 million people took part in antiwar marches in up to 60 different countries.[4]

Many protesters carried signs saying "No Blood for Oil" and claimed that the main reason for the war was to protect Western oil companies. The protesters insisted that there was no proof that Iraq was creating WMDs. They declared that it was against international law to invade another country, even if its leader was corrupt. Protesters also expressed outrage that the war would lead to thousands of innocent lives being lost.

Despite many protests against the war, the U.S. government continued to gather support for its invasion plans. By March 2003, 49 countries had responded to U.S. pressure and declared that they were in favor of military action.[5] Of this total, however, only four nations (the United Kingdom, Australia, Poland, and Denmark) contributed troops to the invasion force.[6] This small group was in stark contrast to the force of 34 nations that fought in the First Gulf

War, and it reflected widespread doubts about whether an invasion of Iraq could really be justified.

PREPARING TO INVADE

As early as the summer of 2002, the U.S. government had started making plans for an invasion. In October the government authorized the use of U.S. forces against Iraq,[7] and by January 2003 a secret invasion date had been fixed for March.[8] This timetable for war was followed very closely, despite the lack of evidence for WMDs.

On March 16, Bush and Blair held an emergency meeting with the presidents of Spain and Portugal, on the Portuguese island of the Azores. The four leaders discussed whether war with Iraq could be avoided, but they reached the conclusion that they should move forward with their preparations to invade.[9] The next day, President Bush gave Saddam and his sons 48 hours to leave Iraq or face war.[10] Two days later, Bush made his official declaration of war, announcing that "diplomacy had failed" and he would therefore proceed with a "Coalition of the willing" to rid Iraq of its WMDs.[11] The invasion of Iraq was officially launched on March 20, 2003.[12]

BIOGRAPHY

Tony Blair

BORN: Edinburgh, Scotland, 1953

ROLE: Prime minister of the United Kingdom, 1997–2007

Tony Blair studied at Oxford University before working as a lawyer. At the age of 30, he was elected to parliament, the UK law-making body, and in 1994 he became leader of the **Labour Party**. Blair was elected prime minister in 1997, at age 43. Following the 9/11 attacks, he supported President Bush in his policy of a "war on terror," ordering UK troops into war in Afghanistan and Iraq. After the Second Gulf War he lost popularity, as many people blamed him for using dishonest methods to help start the war. He resigned as prime minister in 2007.[13]

A WAR ON LAND

The Second Gulf War relied heavily on troops on the ground. Unlike the First Gulf War, which began with a massive air campaign, the invasion of Iraq was mainly fought on land, with support from the air. The Coalition armies faced a dangerous challenge as they advanced from their base in Kuwait to the south of Iraq. Their forces had to cover more than 300 miles (480 kilometers) before they reached Baghdad, Iraq's capital city.

The Coalition forces could rely on state-of-the-art equipment and weapons and superbly trained troops, but their numbers were much smaller than in the First Gulf War. It has been estimated that the Coalition invasion force in 2003 totaled around 170,000[14] (compared with 800,000 in 1990[15]). Saddam's army was also much smaller than in the First Gulf War, numbering between 150,000 and 200,000[16] (compared with around a million men in 1990[17]). Apart from the well-trained Republican Guard of around 60,000 men,[18] the Iraqi army in 2003 was largely made up of conscripts. Saddam's troops were weak and demoralized, and their equipment was out-of-date. Nevertheless, the Coalition generals prepared for a difficult campaign.

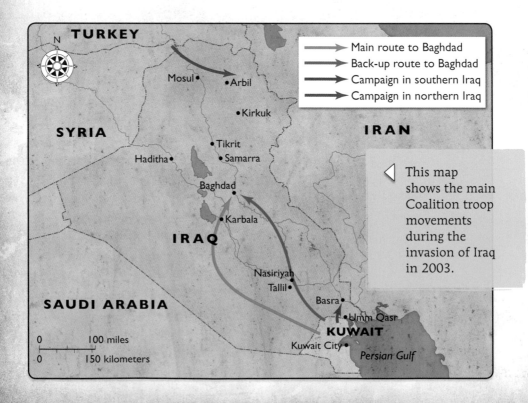

Main route to Baghdad
Back-up route to Baghdad
Campaign in southern Iraq
Campaign in northern Iraq

TURKEY
N
Mosul • • Arbil
• Kirkuk
SYRIA
IRAN
• Tikrit
Haditha • • Samarra
Baghdad •
• Karbala
IRAQ
Nasiriyah
Tallil •
Basra •
SAUDI ARABIA
• Umm Qasr
KUWAIT
Kuwait City •
Persian Gulf

0   100 miles
0   150 kilometers

This map shows the main Coalition troop movements during the invasion of Iraq in 2003.

The Second Gulf War began with a combined air, land, and sea attack on the Al-Faw peninsula, in the southeast corner of Iraq. By March 25, U.S. and Polish forces had captured the port of Umm Qasr.[19] Meanwhile, UK units gained control of oil fields in southern Iraq.

While the campaign was being waged in the south, U.S. and UK tank units were advancing northward toward Baghdad. This huge advance had been carefully planned, with prearranged stops for refueling, so that the tanks would barely halt in their progress. At the same time, in northern Iraq, a special task force consisting of U.S. troops and Kurdish forces was securing the cities of Mosul and Kirkuk and the oil fields of the north.

By early April, Coalition forces had captured the key airfields of Nasiriyah and Tallil. These key objectives were not easily achieved, and fighting in Nasiriyah was especially fierce. Eventually, though, U.S. troops managed to secure the Karbala Gap, the main approach to Baghdad from the south, and Coalition troops began to pour into the city.[20]

THE FALL OF BAGHDAD

On April 9, the Coalition gained control of Baghdad.[21] The city's dramatic capture was greeted by widespread rejoicing, but this was rapidly followed by violence and looting (stealing). For a few days after the fall of Baghdad, fighting continued in other parts of Iraq, but Coalition troops met little resistance. On April 13, they captured the town of Tikrit, close to Saddam's birthplace.[22] Tikrit had been seen as Saddam's last stronghold, and once it had been taken it was clear that the Coalition had gained control of Iraq.

MISSION ACCOMPLISHED?

On May 2, 2003, President Bush delivered a televised speech from the deck of the U.S. aircraft carrier USS *Abraham Lincoln*. He stood in front of a large banner saying "Mission Accomplished" and announced the end of major combat operations in Iraq.[23] In fact, the Coalition's problems had only just begun. Saddam and his sons had not yet been captured, and the invading troops still faced resistance in many parts of Iraq. The Coalition also faced the daunting task of establishing a new Iraqi government, as well as attempting to rebuild a shattered nation.

FALL OF BAGHDAD

As U.S. tanks began to roll into Baghdad, there was an atmosphere of both excitement and terror in the city. Some people gathered at the roadside to cheer the troops, while excited young Iraqis fired ammunition at posters of Saddam. However, many more Iraqis stayed away, fearing to show their support for the invasion in case Saddam would triumph after all. There was also a desperate attempt to get away from the fighting. Thousands of people poured out of the city, driving trucks and cars piled high with their possessions.

SUPPORT AND BETRAYAL

Within a few days of their arrival in Baghdad, it was clear that the Coalition forces were unstoppable. On April 4, they gained control of the airport and began moving in on the city.[24] However, despite these advances, Saddam's loyal (or terrified) supporters were still determined to put up a fight. On the night the airport was captured, the Iraqi information minister, Mohammed Saeed al-Sahhaf, appeared on television to deny that Coalition troops were within 100 miles (160 kilometers) of Baghdad.[25] These ridiculous claims led the international press to call him Comical Ali (a twist on the nickname of another of Saddam's ministers, known as Chemical Ali). Other supporters of Saddam showed their hatred of the Americans by launching desperate suicide-bomb attacks. Yet the majority of Saddam's government and army simply melted away. After the fall of Baghdad, Saddam was reported as saying: "I trusted the commanders, but they were traitors, and they betrayed Iraq."[26]

Stolen treasures

In the chaos following the fall of Baghdad, people seized the chance to steal priceless treasures from the city's museum. The director of the Iraqi National Museum reported that looters had taken or destroyed around 170,000 items, carrying them away in cars and wheelbarrows.[27]

Ali's story

For 12-year-old Ali Abbas, the bombing raids on Baghdad had tragic consequences. On March 30, 2003, a missile from a U.S. plane missed its military target and hit his house in a southern suburb of Baghdad. The house collapsed in a mass of flames, burying Ali and his family. Ali was pulled from the burning wreckage, but his parents and his younger brother did not survive. Ali had terrible burns. His arms were just two blackened stumps, and his chest and back were covered with blisters. At the hospital, the doctors did what they could to save his life. They amputated both his arms, treated his burns, and waited to see if he would live. Over the next few days, the battle for Baghdad raged around the hospital, and Ali's condition grew worse.

Ali would have certainly died if a Western news team had not told his story. Soon his face was appearing on television screens and newspapers around the world. An international campaign was launched to save Ali's life, and on April 16, he was moved to a hospital in Kuwait City. There he received expert care for the next four months, before traveling to the United Kingdom to be fitted with artificial arms. Today, Ali lives in London and is hopeful about his future, but he will never forget the night the bombs fell over Baghdad.[28]

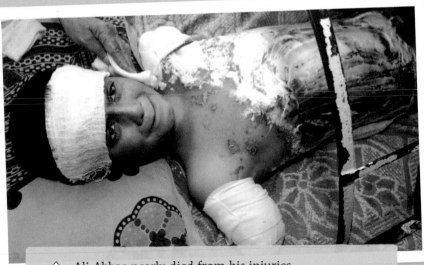

⚠ Ali Abbas nearly died from his injuries.

AFTERMATH

In the months that followed the fall of Baghdad, a temporary government was put in place by the Coalition. The aim of this transitional government was to rule Iraq until it was possible for the Iraqis to hold a general election and elect their own government. At the same time, Coalition troops undertook the task of maintaining order in Iraq. However, they faced growing resistance to their presence. At first, this opposition came mainly from members of the Ba'ath Party, who had once supported Saddam. Soon, though, other groups were expressing their anger at the foreign soldiers who were occupying their country.

TROOPS UNDER ATTACK

Rebel groups known as **insurgents** used a range of methods to attack Coalition troops, including shooting, bombing, and surprise ambushes on army vehicles. Many of the rebels were equipped with missiles, bombs, and guns that had once belonged to the Iraqi army. Fighting often took place in city streets, where Coalition soldiers found it very hard to defend themselves. Rebel attacks grew more frequent during the fall of 2003, as a group of insurgents

Where's the plan?

Once the invasion was over, it soon became clear that the Coalition had no clear plan for restoring order to Iraq. It had failed to achieve its objective of regime change (replacing an old government with a new one). Instead, it had simply brought down Saddam's regime and failed to replace it with a workable new government. As the months went past, it also became evident that the Coalition had seriously underestimated the time it would take to rebuild Iraq. Before the campaign began, U.S. commanders predicted that after the fighting was over there would be a two- to three-month "stabilization" phase, followed by an 18- to 24-month "recovery" stage.[1] In fact, the struggle to create a peaceful and well-run nation still continues today.

launched a determined campaign, known as the Ramadan Offensive.[2] In response, Coalition forces began to use air power and heavy weapons for the first time since the invasion.

One of the main tasks for Coalition troops was to track down Saddam and his sons, Uday and Qusay. In July 2003, his sons were killed by U.S. troops in a gun battle, along with his 14-year-old grandson.[3] In December 2003, Saddam himself was captured in a surprise raid known as Operation Red Dawn.[4]

△ This shows Saddam Hussein soon after his capture. Saddam's trial took over a year, and he was found guilty of crimes against humanity.

Following Saddam's capture, the number of insurgent attacks fell—at least for a while. Training began for Iraqi security forces to take over the role of policing their country. At the same time, money from Iraq's oil sales was used to start the process of rebuilding the country's schools, hospitals, and other services.

TROUBLE GROWS

In the year following the fall of Baghdad, some progress was made toward a return to normal life, but most Iraqis still suffered terrible living conditions. There was widespread lack of food, and people had to cope with frequent power failures and water shortages. The Iraqis had hoped for real improvements after the invasion, and they felt angry and let down. There were also violent clashes between different groups within Iraq. Once the Iraqi people were freed from the control of Saddam's rule, all the old divisions between religions and races flared up again.

By the spring of 2004, violence in Iraq was on the increase.[5] Conflict between Sunnis and Shi'as was becoming more intense, while rebels within Iraq were backed by organized groups from other parts of the Middle East. There were even claims that al-Qaeda was organizing attacks on U.S. troops. At the same time, a massive bombing campaign was directed at the newly formed Iraqi security forces.

HORRORS AND OUTRAGE

In April 2004, severe violence broke out in the mainly Sunni city of Fallujah, in central Iraq.[6] The First Battle of Fallujah (code named Operation Vigilant Resolve by the Coalition) followed a shocking event involving four private U.S. citizens. The four men worked for Blackwater, a company that supplied security guards for the U.S. Army in Iraq, and on March 31, they were killed by rebels who ambushed their trucks. After the killing, local people dragged the four bodies from the trucks, beat them and set them on fire, and then hung two of the corpses over a bridge.[7]

When photos of the Blackwater corpses appeared in the Western press, there was widespread outrage. This prompted Coalition commanders to wage the First Battle of Fallujah, in an attempt to make the city safer. When this attempt failed, a second battle was waged in November 2004.[8] The Second Battle of Fallujah (code named Operation Phantom Fury) lasted for 46 days and ended in a Coalition victory—but not before more than 1,200 insurgents had died[9] and the city of Fallujah was left in ruins.

Another major news story hit the headlines in April 2004, when photos were released from inside the prisoner-of-war camp at Abu Ghraib. These pictures showed U.S. soldiers torturing Iraqi prisoners and mocking their Muslim faith.[10]

The horrific images from Abu Ghraib had a dramatic impact on public opinion. Inside Iraq, the insurgents stepped up their campaign against U.S. troops. In the wider world, there was an enormous drop in support for the Coalition occupation of Iraq. The soldiers who took part in the disturbing events at Abu Ghraib were tried and punished, but people did not forget their cruelty. There were also some cases of British troops mistreating Iraqis.[11]

Faced with incidents such as the torture at Abu Ghraib, some Iraqis questioned whether the Coalition was capable of governing any better than Saddam Hussein. In response to these negative attitudes toward it, the Coalition made renewed efforts to win the support of the Iraqi people. Troops were instructed to try to win the confidence of local people in a campaign known as "hearts and minds." However, this aim proved very hard to achieve.

A CHANGE OF GOVERNMENT

In January 2005, elections were held for an Iraqi Transitional National Assembly.[12] This organization took over from the temporary government that had been put in place by the Coalition. Eleven months later, the Iraqi people voted for a full-term government.[13] The new Iraqi government was installed in May 2006.[14] Its members included Kurds, Sunnis, and Shi'as, led by Prime Minister Nouri al-Maliki, a Shi'a Muslim who had been a passionate opponent of Saddam Hussein.

Blackwater operations

The U.S.-based company Blackwater was founded in 1997 to provide armed security guards in trouble spots around the world. Blackwater had many guards working in Iraq, but the company was placed under investigation after a violent incident that took place in Baghdad in September 2007. In this incident, Blackwater guards shot and killed 17 Iraqi civilians, claiming that they were a threat to security. This was the worst of several occasions in which Blackwater employees seemed to be taking the law into their own hands. Following the investigation, Blackwater was banned from operating in Iraq.[15]

△ Over 900 Blackwater employees worked in Iraq in the period following the fall of Baghdad, and many of them were employed by the U.S. government to guard their officials.

The new Iraqi government faced an incredibly difficult task. During 2005 tensions had increased between Sunnis and Shi'as, as suicide bombers targeted Shi'a gatherings. Then in February 2006, violence between Sunnis and Shi'as erupted following the bombing of the al-Askari Mosque in Samarra, one of the holiest Shi'a sites.[16] In the weeks and months after the bombing, the death toll soared across the country. A UN envoy reported in November that the killings were "tearing apart the political and social fabric of Iraq."[17]

Estimated Iraqi civilian deaths, 2003–2010

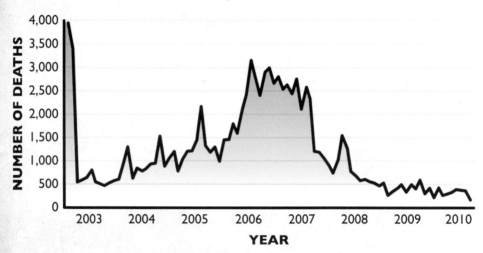

A SUDDEN SURGE

The worsening situation in Iraq prompted a new U.S. policy. In January 2007, President Bush announced that he would send 20,000 more troops to Iraq.[18] The aim of this new plan, known as the "surge," was to solve some of Iraq's outstanding problems before the United States began to withdraw its troops.

The surge was headed by U.S. General David Petraeus, and it seemed to make a difference. In June 2008, the U.S. government reported that violence in Iraq had dropped by between 40 and 80 percent since February 2007,[19] although these figures were questioned by some reporters. The government also claimed that the death rate for Coalition troops had dropped to its lowest level since the start of the war.[20]

Yet despite the successes of the surge, politicians in Iraq and in the United States continued to campaign for a rapid withdrawal of U.S. troops and a change of focus that emphasized protecting the population.

ANBAR AWAKENING

Possibly the most important factor in improving security in Iraq is what is called the "Anbar Awakening," in which Sunni Arab tribal leaders agreed to stop fighting Coalition forces in return for letting them maintain power.

By the spring of 2008, the Iraqi army was playing an active part in defeating insurgent attacks. In Basra province, the UK army deliberately held back while the Iraqis overcame a Shi'a uprising.[21] This successful campaign by the Iraqi forces helped the Iraqis to feel that their people were finally gaining control of their nation's destiny. In March 2009, the United Kingdom began withdrawing its troops from the region, and the last UK troops left Iraq on July 31, 2009.[22] In February 2009, the new U.S. president, Barack Obama, announced a deadline of the end of August 2010 for withdrawing combat troops from Iraq.[23]

On August 19, 2010, the last U.S. combat unit left Iraq. This put an end to Operation Iraqi Freedom, which had begun seven years before with the invasion of Iraq.[24] The next stage of the U.S. mission was code named Operation New Dawn. This operation involved about 50,000 troops who remained in Iraq to train, equip, and advise the Iraqi army. Operation New Dawn is scheduled to run until the end of 2011.[25]

Invisible wounds

Soldiers who have recently returned from Iraq are thrilled to be home, but they face a difficult future as they struggle to cope with their memories of the horror of war. According to Scott Swaim, a Gulf War veteran and therapist, troops that come home initially experience "the honeymoon period," but then they are hit by a range of "emotional challenges," including depression, isolation, stress, and anger. Swaim warns that suicide rates for Gulf War veterans are "off the charts." In the years 2005 to 2009, more than 1,000 members of the U.S. armed forces committed suicide.[26] In 2010 the U.S. armed services reported 434 suicides on active duty, a figure that exceeded the number of deaths in battle.[27]

LIFE IN IRAQ

What is life like in Iraq, now that all the combat troops have left? For most Iraqi citizens, life has become much calmer during the last couple of years. No one has forgotten the desperate days of 2006–2008, when people lived in fear of shootings, bombings, and kidnappings, but they are beginning to rebuild their lives.

LIFE IN BAGHDAD

In December 2010, a reporter interviewed some citizens of Baghdad. One of the people he spoke to was Salman, a Shi'a storeowner, who lived in the Sunni residential area of Dora.[28] In 2006 Salman and his family had been driven out of their neighborhood by hostile Sunni groups, but they had recently returned and Salman had opened up his store again.

▷ Against all odds, normal life continues in Iraq.

Better under Saddam?

Violence in Iraq reached its peak between 2006 and 2008. A UN report from this period compared the situation in Baghdad to a civil war.[29] During the years of violence, a number of Iraqis claimed that they had been better off under Saddam. Today, far fewer people make this claim, but some Iraqi women disagree. They say that they do not have the same freedom that they had in Saddam's time.

Salman reported that in recent months his customers had finally felt safe enough to stay and catch up with each other in his store. However, there were still tensions in his neighborhood. Farther down the street, an armored military vehicle was parked outside a Christian family's house, to give them some protection after recent attacks.

THE CHILDREN OF BASRA

During the last three years, life in the port of Basra in southwest Iraq has gradually returned to normal. Children have begun to play in the streets, stores and restaurants have reopened, and building projects have started in some parts of the city.

Today, Basra is a city of children. So many adults were killed in wars over the past 30 years that children now make up 50 percent of the city's total population. Many of them have taken on the role of wage-earner for their family. Others are orphans, living in orphanages or surviving on their own on the streets.

In an interview for the newspaper *The Observer*,[30] some of Basra's children described their lives. Twelve-year-old Taha has a disabled father, so he collects aluminum cans and sells them for recycling. He works for more than 12 hours a day to earn enough money to support his family. Sabeha is also 12 years old and lives in an orphanage. She feels she is lucky to be able to play and study, and she is remarkably positive about her life, saying: "My life is developing well and so is Basra. Everywhere I go outside I see new buildings, different colors, new parks, green grass, and restaurants. I want this to be a future for all Iraq."

WHAT HAVE WE LEARNED?

What lessons have been learned from the wars in the Gulf? One thing at least is clear. When foreign leaders try to make changes in a country, they cannot expect events to work out as they had planned.

MAKING MISTAKES

The Coalition leaders made some serious mistakes, especially during the Second Gulf War. In 2003 they invaded Iraq without making sure their reasons for war were legal and just. They went ahead with the invasion in the face of widespread opposition from other countries and from within their own countries. They also failed to make adequate plans for the period following the invasion. While the Coalition soon achieved its aim of deposing Saddam, this proved to be just the start of years of conflict, involving thousands of casualties. Instead of restoring peace and order, Coalition troops struggled to keep control of a country torn apart by ethnic divisions. Indeed, many experts argue that the presence of Western troops was a major cause of violence in Iraq in the years after 2003.

Unlike the second war in the Gulf, the First Gulf War was seen by many people as a just war because it drove Saddam out of a country

Casualties of war: First Gulf War

Numbers for Coalition deaths in combat are exact, but there has been much dispute about the numbers of Iraqis killed during the First Gulf War.

- 148 U.S. troops
- 99 troops from other Coalition nations
- between 20,000 and 56,000 Iraqi troops
- between 1,000 and 3,500 Iraqi civilians.[1]

he had invaded. It was over quickly, and there were few casualties on the Coalition's side. Iraqi deaths, however, totaled more than 30,000, and Coalition commanders faced strong criticism for their attacks on retreating Iraqi troops on the Highway of Death. Despite these criticisms, the Coalition generally had public opinion on its side during the First Gulf War.

LEARNING LESSONS?

Faced with a problem like Saddam's Iraq, governments in the future might try to improve international cooperation to put pressure on regimes. This might help to ensure military action is undertaken only in the case of an undeniable security threat. However, events in Libya, where Colonel Muammar Gaddafi runs a corrupt regime that has been compared to that of Saddam, have proved that foreign powers will still take military action quickly in the hope that they can remove a dangerous dictator.

Following the scandal of the false evidence for WMDs, governments will need to make sure that their reasons for war are sound and legal. Eight years after the Iraq War was launched, the ex-UK prime minister, Tony Blair, faced the Chilcot Enquiry, a public investigation into the legality of his actions. However, President Obama has not pushed for similar investigations into the legality of decisions taken by ex-President Bush. It is hoped that future governments will learn lessons from the Iraq War and will not be so willing to rely on evidence provided by questionable sources.

Governments may also learn from the problems encountered in Iraq after the invasion. If a change of regime is attempted in the future, plans need to be made for establishing a replacement government. Any replacement regime would need to have the widespread support of the country's populations, in order for the people to feel they are really being offered a better future.

Casualties of war: Second Gulf War

Estimated deaths in combat from the start of the war on March 20, 2003, to October 10, 2010, are:

- 4,744 Coalition troops
- 150,726 Iraqis (civilians, insurgents, and Iraqi soldiers).[2]

TIMELINE

1958 The Iraqi army seizes control of the country. The royal family is expelled and Iraq becomes a republic.

1968 The Ba'ath Party takes control in Iraq. General Ahmad Hassan al-Bakr is made president and Saddam Hussein deputy president.

April 1979 An Islamic revolution in Iran replaces the Shah (king) with the Shi'a cleric Ayatollah Khomeini.

July 1979 Saddam becomes president of Iraq.

September 1980 Iraqi troops invade Iran, starting the eight-year Iran-Iraq War.

1982 The United States removes Iraq from its list of State Sponsors of Terrorism and gives Saddam open support in the Iran-Iraq War.

1986 The Anfal campaign against the Kurds begins. It lasts three years.

March 1988 The Kurdish town of Halabja is attacked with chemical weapons.

August 1988 The Iran-Iraq War ends.

August 2, 1990 Iraq invades Kuwait. UN Resolution 660 condemns the invasion and demands that Iraqi troops withdraw from Kuwait.

August 6, 1990 Planning begins for Operation Desert Shield. UN Resolution 661 places international trade sanctions on Iraq.

August 8, 1990 Saddam makes his cousin Ali Hassan al-Majid the governor of Kuwait.

November 1990 UN Resolution 678 gives Iraq a deadline of January 15, 1991, to withdraw from Kuwait.

January 16, 1991 Coalition forces launch a four-week-long bombing campaign over Kuwait and Iraq.

January 29, 1991 The battle of Al Khafji is fought in Saudi Arabia. It is a victory for the Coalition.

February 24, 1991 The Coalition ground campaign, code named Operation Desert Sabre, begins.

February 27, 1991 Saddam orders a retreat from Kuwait City. The retreating Iraqi troops are heavily bombarded by Coalition forces.

February 28, 1991 President Bush orders a cease-fire. The First Gulf War ends.

1992 Operation Southern Watch is put into place, with a no-fly zone for Iraqi planes established over south Iraq.

1993 U.S. forces launch a missile attack on Baghdad following claims that Saddam had plotted to assassinate President Bush.

October 1995 Saddam wins a referendum allowing him to remain as president for another seven years.

August 1996 Iraqi forces invade the Kurdish regions of northern Iraq. U.S. forces respond by launching Operation Desert Strike.

December 1996 The UN puts into operation an "Oil for Food" program in an attempt to ease the economic problems in Iraq.

October 1998 Iraq ends cooperation with UNSCOM weapons inspectors.

December 1998 The United States and the United Kingdom launch Operation Desert Fox, with the aim of destroying Iraq's WMD programs.

1999 The UN creates UNMOVIC to replace UNSCOM.

February 2001 The United States and United Kingdom launch bombing raids to try to disable Iraq's air defense network.

September 11, 2001 Terrorists attack the World Trade Center's twin towers in New York City and the Pentagon in Washington, D.C.

October 2001 Coalition forces, led by the United States and the United Kingdom, go to war with Afghanistan.

September 2002 U.S. President George W. Bush warns world leaders of the "grave and gathering danger" of Iraq. UK Prime Minister Tony Blair publishes a questionable dossier on Iraq's military capability.

October 2002 The U.S. government authorizes the use of U.S. forces against Iraq.

November 2002 UN weapons inspectors, led by Hans Blix, return to Iraq.

January 2003 Public protests against war in Iraq are held in Western countries.

February 2003 U.S. Secretary of State Colin Powell presents evidence to the UN that Iraq is producing WMDs.

March 7, 2003 Hans Blix reports that he needs more time in Iraq.

March 17, 2003 UN weapons inspectors leave Iraq. Bush gives Saddam and his sons 48 hours to leave Iraq or face war.

March 19, 2003 Bush makes an official declaration of war.

March 20, 2003 The Coalition invasion of Iraq begins.

April 9, 2003 Coalition troops gain control of Baghdad.

May 2003 A U.S.-led temporary administration is set up in Iraq and UN trade sanctions are lifted.

July 2003 Saddam's sons, Uday and Qusay, are killed in a gun battle.

October 2003 The Ramadan Offensive is launched by insurgents. The Iraq Survey Group reports that it has found no WMDs and no viable WMD program.

December 2003 Saddam is captured by U.S. troops.

March 2004 Suicide bombers attack Shi'a festivals in Karbala and Baghdad.

April 2004 First Battle of Fallujah, a month-long U.S. siege of the city. Photos are published of Abu Ghraib prison, showing abuses of Iraqi prisoners by U.S. troops.

November 2004 Second Battle of Fallujah. It lasts for 46 days and ends in a U.S. victory.

January 2005 Elections are held for an Iraqi Transitional National Assembly.

December 2005 Elections are held for an Iraqi government and parliament.

February 2006 Violence between Sunnis and Shi'as erupts following the bombing of the al-Askari Mosque in Samarra.

December 2006 Saddam Hussein is executed for crimes against humanity.

January 2007 Bush's "surge" strategy sends 20,000 more troops to Iraq.

2007 The United Kingdom hands over security of the southern province of Basra to Iraqi forces.

2008 The United States hands over control of the western province of Anbar to the Iraqi government.

2009 U.S. President Barack Obama announces the withdrawal of U.S. combat troops by the end of August 2010.

July 2009 A majority of UK troops leaves Iraq.

January 2010 Ali Hassan al-Majid, (Chemical Ali) is executed.

August 2010 The last U.S. combat unit leaves Iraq. Operation Iraqi Freedom ends, and Operation New Dawn begins. This aims to complete the process of training, equipping, and advising the Iraqi army.

October 2010 The website Wikileaks publishes secret documents on the Iraq War.

February 2011 Rafid Ahmed Alwan al-Janabi (code name Curveball) admits that evidence he supplied to the Coalition for the existence of WMDs was false.

May 2011 The last UK troops, who were training the Iraqi navy, leave Iraq.

GLOSSARY

alliance friendship and cooperation between nations

al-Qaeda Islamic terrorist group based in Afghanistan, led by Osama bin Laden. Al-Qaeda was responsible for the attacks on the World Trade Center in New York City and the Pentagon in Washington, D.C., on September 11, 2001.

ambassador someone who holds an official position in a foreign country, as a representative of his or her own government

ammunition bullets or missiles that can be fired by a weapon

assassinate deliberately kill a public figure

Ba'ath Party political party in Iraq that aims to create a socially equal, modern society. Ba'ath Party members are against religious extremism, but in favor of Arab nationalism, and wish to free all Arab nations from control by Western countries.

biological weapon gas, spray, or powder containing germs that cause deadly diseases and can kill people in large numbers

call sign code name used in communications

chemical weapon gas, spray, or powder containing chemical poison that can injure or kill people in very large numbers—for example, mustard gas and cyanide gas

CIA U.S. secret service, responsible for spies and secret agents in the United States and abroad. The initials "CIA" stand for "Central Intelligence Agency."

coalition group of nations (or politicians) working together

Democrat someone who belongs to the Democratic political party in the United States. Democrats tend to lean center-left to progressive in U.S. politics.

deport force someone to leave a country

depose remove someone by force from a position of power

ethnic relating to people's race

human rights abuse any action that has the result of denying people basic rights to freedom of action and freedom of speech. Human rights abuses often involve imprisoning, torturing, and even killing people.

insurgent someone who rebels against a government or another controlling power

Islamic revolution revolution that aims to create a Muslim society with Muslim laws and traditions

Kurds race of people who have lived for centuries in an area now covered by parts of Iraq, Iran, Syria, and Turkey. Most Iraqi Kurds live in the north of the country.

Labour Party UK political party whose members aim to create a more equal society. Labour Party members traditionally believe in state support for the underprivileged.

land mine bomb that is buried in the ground and explodes if someone walks on it or touches a tripwire

militant ready to use extreme methods, such as violence, to achieve an aim

military dictator ruler of a country who is also the head of its armed forces and who rules through fear

missile weapon that travels through the air to its target

mobilize prepare fighting forces for action

nationalist someone who feels passionately loyal to his or her country and believes it should be free of foreign control

naval blockade block to shipping created and policed by large ships from a country's navy

nerve gas gas that prevents the nerves from sending messages to the body's organs and causes death by suffocation

no-fly zone area of airspace where planes are not allowed to fly

nuclear reactor factory that produces nuclear power

nuclear weapon weapon created from nuclear energy that can produce an enormous explosion—for example, bombs or missiles

Ottoman belonging to the Ottoman Turks. They ruled an enormous empire from the 15th century to the end of World War I.

persecution very cruel and unfair treatment of an individual, a group, or a race. Persecution often involves violence.

province large region of a country or an empire, with its own government

republic country or a state that does not have a monarchy (king or queen)

Republican someone who belongs to the Republican political party in the United States. Republicans tend to lean center-right to conservative in U.S. politics.

resolution announcement of a decision that has been made by a group of people

SAS Special Air Service, a branch of the UK forces that conducts unusual and often very dangerous operations

satellite technology ways of communicating or finding directions (such as cell phones and navigation devices) that use signals beamed from satellites in space

Scud missile very large surface-to-surface missile that can travel more than 200 miles (320 kilometers) and cause serious damage

secular non-religious

Shi'a Muslim who belongs to the Shi'a sect (group)

smart bombs missiles with a built-in navigation device that allows them to hit a target with great accuracy. Smart bombs are also called precision guided missiles.

Sunni Muslim who belongs to the Sunni sect (group)

trade sanction ban on trade with a nation, in order to put pressure on that nation's leaders to change the way they rule

United Nations (UN) organization of nations, formed in 1945, to promote peace, security, and international cooperation

UNSCOM organization set up by the UN to check that Saddam was not hiding or producing weapons of mass destruction. The full title of UNSCOM is "the United Nations Special Commission to Oversee the Destruction of Iraq's Weapons of Mass Destruction."

weapons of mass destruction (WMDs) chemical, biological, or nuclear weapons that can kill or injure very large numbers of people

Wikileaks organization that publishes on the Internet information that was previously private or secret. The information is "leaked" to Wikileaks by a range of anonymous sources.

NOTES ON SOURCES

Saddam's Iraq (pages 6–13)

1. "Saddam Hussein," *Encyclopædia Britannica*, http://library.eb.co.uk/eb/article-284496. Accessed on February 20, 2011.
2. "Oil in Iraq: The Byzantine Beginnings," *Global Policy Forum*. Accessed on April 3, 2011.
3. Derek Hopwood, "British Relations with Iraq," Iraq: Conflict in Context, BBC Recent History, http://www.bbc.co.uk/history/recent/iraq/britain_iraq_02.shtml. Accessed on February 20, 2011; "Background Note: Iraq," U.S. State Department, http://www.state.gov/r/pa/ei/bgn/6804.htm#history. Accessed on February 20, 2011.
4. "Iraq," CIA World Factbook, https://www.cia.gov/library/publications/the-world-factbook/geos/iz.html. Accessed on February 20, 2011.
5. *Ibid.*
6. "Saddam Hussein," *Encyclopædia Britannica*.
7. Jean Sasson, *Mayada: Daughter of Iraq* (New York: Dutton, 2003).
8. Zainab Salbi and Laurie Becklund, *Hidden in Plain Sight, Growing Up in the Shadow of Saddam* (London: Vision, 2005).
9. John Simpson, *The Wars Against Saddam: Taking the Hard Road to Baghdad* (London: Macmillan, 2003), 51.
10. "Iraq's Brutal Decrees: Amputation, Branding and the Death Penalty," Human Rights Watch, June 1, 1995, available at www.unhcr.org/refworld/docid/3ae6a7f00.html. Accessed on February 20, 2011.

War and Tyranny (pages 14–19)

1. "The Iranian Revolution," International Relations, *Encyclopædia Britannica*, http://library.eb.co.uk/eb/article-32981. Accessed April 3, 2011.
2. "Iran Hostage Crisis," *Encyclopædia Britannica*, http://library.eb.co.uk/eb/article-248557. Accessed on April 3, 2011.
3. "Iran-Iraq War," *Encyclopædia Britannica*, http://library.eb.co.uk/eb/article-9042742. Accessed on February 20, 2011.
4. "Iran-Iraq War," *Encyclopædia Britannica*; "Saddam's Iraq: Key Events: Western support 1980–88: Iran-Iraq War 1980–1988," BBC News, http://news.bbc.co.uk/1/shared/spl/hi/middle_east/02/iraq_events/html/western_support.stm. Accessed on February 20, 2011.
5. "Western Support 1980-88: Iran-Iraq War 1980–1988," BBC News.
6. "Anfal: Campaign Against the Kurds," BBC News, June 24, 2007, http://news.bbc.co.uk/1/hi/world/middle_east/4877364.stm. Accessed on February 20, 2011.
7. "Genocide in Iraq: The Anfal Campaign Against the Kurds," Human Rights Watch, July 1993, http://www.hrw.org/legacy/reports/1993/iraqanfal/#Table%20of. Accessed on February 20, 2011.

8. "1988: Thousands Die in Halabja Gas Attack," BBC On This Day, March 16, 1988, http://news.bbc.co.uk/onthisday/hi/dates/stories/march/16/newsid_4304000/4304853.stm. Accessed on February 20, 2011.
9. "Gulf War," *New World Encyclopedia*, http://www.newworldencyclopedia.org/entry/Gulf_War. Accessed on July 8, 2011.
10. John Simpson, *The Wars Against Saddam*, 83-88.
11. "Genocide in Iraq: The Anfal Campaign Against the Kurds," Introduction.

Invading Kuwait (pages 20–27)

1. "Iran-Iraq War," *Encyclopædia Britannica*.
2. "Iran-Iraq War (1980–1988)," GlobalSecurity.org, http://www.globalsecurity.org/military/world/war/iran-iraq.htm. Accessed on February 20, 2011.
3. "Iran-Iran War 1980–1988," BBC News.
4. John Keegan, *The Iraq War: The 21 Day Conflict and its Aftermath* (London: Pimlico, 2004), 69.
5. "Kuwait," *Encyclopedia of the Nations*, http://www.country-data.com/cgi-bin/query/r-7600.html. Accessed on February 20, 2011.
6. *Ibid.*
7. *Ibid.*
8. Patrick Cockburn, "Beware Your Enemy's Stupidity," *The Independent*, January 5, 2011, http://www.independent.co.uk/opinion/commentators/patrick-cockburn-beware-your-enemys-stupidity-2175956.html#. Accessed on February 20, 2011.
9. Alastair Finlan, *Essential Histories: The Gulf War 1991* (Oxford: Osprey, 2003), 25.
10. *Ibid*, 25–26.
11. *Ibid*, 26.
12. *Ibid.*
13. *Ibid.*
14. *Ibid.*
15. *Ibid.*
16. John Bulloch and Harvey Morris, *Saddam's War: The Origins of the Kuwait Conflict and the International Response* (London, Faber and Faber, 1991), 107.
17. *Ibid*, 106–7.
18. "Profile: 'Chemical Ali,'" BBC News.
19. Two interesting eye-witness accounts are provided in: Fred L. Hart, *The Iraqi Invasion of Kuwait*, and Alastair Finlan, *The Gulf War 1991*, 78–80.
20. Jenn Cameroon, "When Our Flag Lost Its Sky ... and Only Hearts Remembered," *Arab Times*, http://www.arabtimesonline.com/NewsDetails/tabid/96/smid/414/ArticleID/157601/reftab/36/Default.aspx. Accessed on February 20, 2011.
21. *Ibid.*
22. *Ibid.*
23. *Ibid*; "UK Hostages Describe Kuwait Ordeal," BBC News, October 16, 2006, http://news.bbc.co.uk/1/hi/uk_politics/6055048.stm. Accessed on February 20, 2011.

First Gulf War (pages 28–35)

1. UN Security Council Resolution 660: Iraq-Kuwait (August 2, 1990), http://daccess-dds-ny.un.org/doc/RESOLUTION/GEN/NR0/575/10/IMG/NR057510.pdf?OpenElement. Accessed on February 20, 2011.
2. Alastair Finlan, *The Gulf War 1991*, 29.
3. *Ibid*.
4. "George Herbert Walker Bush," Biography.com, http://www.biography.com/articles/George-Herbert-Walker-Bush-38066. Accessed on February 20, 2011.
5. UN Security Council Resolution 661: Iraq-Kuwait (August 6, 1990), http://daccess-dds-ny.un.org/doc/RESOLUTION/GEN/NR0/575/10/IMG/NR057510.pdf?OpenElement. Accessed on February 20, 2011.
6. "UNSCOM and the Iraqi Biological Weapons Program," Weapons of Mass Destruction, GlobalSecurity.org, http://www.globalsecurity.org/wmd/world/iraq/bw-unscom.htm. Accessed on February 20, 2011.
7. Martin Chulov, "Iraq Goes Nuclear with Plans for New Reactor Programme," *The Guardian*, October 27, 2009, http://www.guardian.co.uk/world/2009/oct/27/iraq-nuclear-reactor-programme. Accessed on February 20, 2011.
8. UN Security Council Resolution 678: Iraq-Kuwait (November 29, 1990), http://daccess-dds-ny.un.org/doc/RESOLUTION/GEN/NR0/575/15/IMG/NR057515.pdf?OpenElement. Accessed on February 20, 2011.
9. "Gulf War Facts," CNN In-depth Archive, http://web.archive.org/web/20080612131747rn_1/www.cnn.com/SPECIALS/2001/gulf.war/facts/gulfwar/. Accessed on February 20, 2011.
10. Alastair Finlan, *The Gulf War 1991*, 34–35
11. "Gulf War Facts," CNN In-depth Archive.
12. Andy McNab, *Bravo Two Zero: The True Story of an SAS Patrol Behind Enemy Lines in Iraq* (London: Corgi, 1994).
13. Scott Peterson, "'Smarter' Bombs Still Hit Civilians," *Christian Science Moniter*, October 22, 2002, http://www.csmoniter.com/2002/1022/p01s01-wosc.html. Acccessed on July 8, 2011.
14. Alastair Finlan, *The Gulf War 1991*, 17.
15. *Ibid*, 19.
16. *Ibid*, 53–57.

Victory at a Cost (pages 36–41)

1. Alastair Finlan, *The Gulf War 1991*, 51–52.
2. *Ibid*, 52.
3. *Ibid*, 57.
4. "Norman Schwarzkopf," *Academy of Achievement*, http://www.achievement.org/autodoc/page/sch0bio-1. Accessed on February 20, 2011.
5. Alastair Finlan, *The Gulf War 1991*, 57; Seymour Hersh, "Overwhelming Force: What Happened in the Final Days of the Gulf War?" *The New Yorker*, May 22, 2000, 49–82, http://cryptome.org/mccaffrey-sh.htm. Accessed on February 20, 2011.
6. "1991: Iraqi Troops Flee Kuwait City," BBC On This Day, February 26, 1991, http://news.bbc.co.uk/onthisday/hi/dates/stories/february/26/newsid_4716000/4716868.stm. Accessed on February 20, 2011.
7. George Bush and Brent Scowcroft, *A World Transformed* (New York: Knopf, 1998).
8. Tahir Husain, *Kuwaiti Oil Fires: Regional Environmental Perspectives* (Oxford: Pergamon, 1995), 68.

9. "1991: Jubilation Follows Gulf War Cease-Fire," BBC On This Day, February 28, 1991, http://news.bbc.co.uk/onthisday/hi/dates/stories/february/28/newsid_2515000/2515289.stm. Accessed on February 20, 2011.
10. "1991 Gulf War Chronology," In the News, Global Security.org, http://www.globalsecurity.org/news/2003/030320-chronology01.htm. Accessed on February 20, 2011.
11. Quoted in Seymour Hersh, "Overwhelming Force."
12. *Ibid*
13. *Ibid*.
14. "Gulf War Illness and the Health of Gulf War Veterans, Scientific Findings and Recommendations," Research Advisory Committee on Gulf War Veterans' Illnesses, http://sph.bu.edu/insider/images/stories/resources/annual_reports/GWI%20and%20Health%20of%20GW%20Veterans_RAC-GWVI%20Report_2008.pdf. Accessed on February 20, 2011.

An Uneasy Peace (pages 42–49)

1. Adel Darwish, "Uday Hussein: Violent Eldest Son of Saddam Hussein," *The Independent*, July 24, 2003, http://www.independent.co.uk/news/obituaries/uday-hussein-548466.html. Accessed on February 20, 2011.
2. Adel Darwish, "Qusay Hussein: Saddam's 'Cold' Second Son and Trusted Deputy," *The Independent*, July 24, 2003, http://www.independent.co.uk/news/obituaries/qusay-hussein-548465.html. Accessed on February 20, 2011.
3. *Ibid*.
4. Report of the UN Security Council Humanitarian Panel in 1999, cited in "Guide to Sanctions," Campaign Against Sanctions in Iraq, http://www.casi.org.uk/guide/problem.html. Accessed on February 20, 2011.
5. "Oil-for-Food," *UN Office of the Iraq Program*, http://www.un.org/Depts/oip/background/index.html. Accessed on February 20, 2011.
6. "Operation Southern Watch," Globalsecurity.org, http://www.globalsecurity.org/military/ops/southern_watch.htm. Accessed on February 20, 2011.
7. *Ibid*.
8. "Desert Fox: 16–19 December 1998," Saddam's Iraq: Key Events, BBC News, http://news.bbc.co.uk/1/shared/spl/hi/middle_east/02/iraq_events/html/desert_fox.stm. Accessed on February 20, 2011.
9. "Timeline: Iraq Weapons Inspections," BBC News, http://news.bbc.co.uk/1/hi/world/middle_east/2167933.stm. Accessed on February 20, 2011.
10. Bruce W. Nelan, William Dowell, Mark Thompson, and Douglas Waller, "Bugging Saddam," *Time*, January 18, 1999, http://www.time.com/time/magazine/article/0,9171,990017,00.html. Accessed on July 9, 2011.
11. "Timeline: Iraq Weapons Inspections," BBC News.
12. Rahimullah Yusufzai, "Face to Face with Osama," *The Guardian*, September 26, 2001, http://www.guardian.co.uk/world/2001/sep/26/afghanistan.terrorism3. Accessed on February 20, 2011.
13. "Full Text: Bin Laden's 'letter to America,'" *Observer Worldview*, November 24, 2002, http://www.guardian.co.uk/world/2002/nov/24/theobserver. Accessed on February 20, 2011.
14. "UNMOVIC: Basic Facts," *UNMOVIC*, http://www.unmovic.org. Accessed on July 9, 2011.
15. "Timeline: Iraq Weapons Inspections," BBC News.
16. *Ibid*.
17. *Ibid*.

18. "Full Text: Blix Address," BBC News, February 14, 2003, http://news.bbc.co.uk/1/hi/world/middle_east/2763653.stm. Accessed on February 20, 2011.

19. "Security Council March 7, 2003, Oral Introduction of the 12th Quarterly Report of UNMOVIC, Executive Chairman Dr. Hans Blix," http://www.un.org/Depts/unmovic/SC7asdelivered.htm. Accessed on February 20, 2011.

20. "Donald Rumsfeld," *Biography.com*, http://www.biography.com/articles/Donald-Rumsfeld-9466907. Accessed on July 9, 2011.

21. "Rumsfeld Foresees Swift Iraq War," BBC News, February 7, 2003, http://news.bbc.co.uk/1/hi/world/middle_east/2738089.stm. Accessed April 3, 2011.

22. "Dick Cheney," *Biography.com*, http://www.biography.com/articles/Dick-Cheney-9246063. Accessed on July 9, 2011.

23. "Cheney Blasts Media on al Qaeda-Iraq Link," CNN Politics, June 18, 2004, http://articles.cnn.com/2004-06-18/politics/cheney.iraq.al.qaeda_1_iraq-and-al-qaeda-al-qaeda-iraq-link-iraq-war?_s=PM:ALLPOLITICS. Accessed on April 3, 2011; "Cheney Asserts Iraq-al Qaeda Link," BBC News, April 6, 2007, http://news.bbc.co.uk/1/hi/6533367.stm. Accessed on April 3, 2011.

24. "Bush's 'evil axis' Comment Stirs Critics," BBC News, February 2, 2002, http://news.bbc.co.uk/1/hi/world/americas/1796034.stm. Accessed on February 20, 2011.

25. "It's Time for War, Bush and Blair Tell Taliban," *The Observer*, October 7, 2001, http://www.guardian.co.uk/world/2001/oct/07/politics.september11. Accessed on February 20, 2011.

26. Anton La Guardia and Toby Harnden, "Saddam 'is months away from a nuclear bomb,'" *The Telegraph*, September 9, 2002, http://www.telegraph.co.uk/news/worldnews/middleeast/iraq/1406736/Saddam-is-months-away-from-a-nuclear-bomb.html. Accessed on February 20, 2011.

27. "President Delivers 'State of the Union,'" The White House, January 28, 2003, http://georgewbush-whitehouse.archives.gov/news/releases/2003/01/print/20030128-19.html. Accessed on February 20, 2011.

28. "In Quotes: Blair and Iraq Weapons," BBC News, September 29, 2004, http://news.bbc.co.uk/1/hi/uk_politics/3054991.stm. Accessed on February 20, 2011.

29. Dana Priest and Walter Pincus, "U.S. 'almost all wrong' on Weapons," *Washington Post*, October 7, 2004, http://www.washingtonpost.com/wp-dyn/articles/A12115-2004Oct6.html. Accessed on February 20, 2011.

30. Helen Pidd, "Curveball Deserves Permanent Exile for WMD Lies, Say Iraq Politicians," *The Guardian*, February 16, 2011, http://www.guardian.co.uk/world/2011/feb/16/curveball-exile-wmd-lies-iraq-politicians. Accessed on February 20, 2011.

Second Gulf War (pages 50–57)

1. "Powell Presents US Case to Security Council of Iraq's Failure to Disarm," UN News Center, http://www.un.org/apps/news/storyAr.asp?NewsID=6079&Cr=iraq&Cr1=inspect. Accessed on February 20, 2011.

2. Nicholas Watt, "War Is the Worst Solution, Warns Chirac," *The Guardian*, February 5, 2003, http://www.guardian.co.uk/politics/2003/feb/05/uk.iraq. Accessed March 30, 2011.

3. "George W. Bush," Biography.com, http://www.biography.com/articles/George-W.-Bush-9232768. Accessed on February 20, 2011.

4. "Millions Join Global Anti-War Protests," BBC News, February 17, 2003, http://news.bbc.co.uk/1/hi/world/europe/2765215.stm. Accessed on February 20, 2011.

5. http://coalition-of-the-willing.co.tv/. Accessed on February 20, 2011.

6. *Ibid.*

7. "Congressional Resolution on Iraq (Passed by House and Senate October 2002)," History News Network, http://hnn.us/articles/1282.html. Accessed on February 20, 2011.

8. "Bush-Blair Iraq War Memo Revealed," BBC News.

9. "President Bush: Monday 'Moment of Truth' for World on Iraq," The White House, March 16, 2003, http://georgewbush-whitehouse.archives.gov/news/releases/2003/03/20030316-3.html. Accessed on March 31, 2011.

10. "Iraq Timeline," BBC News.

11. "Bush Declares War," CNN.com, March 20, 2003, http://edition.cnn.com/2003/US/03/19/sprj.irq.int.bush.transcript/. Accessed on February 20, 2011.

12. "Iraq Timeline," BBC News.

13. "Tony Blair Biography," The Biography Channel, http://www.thebiographychannel.co.uk/biographies/tony-blair.html. Accessed on February 20, 2011;"Tony Blair Biography," Biogs.com, http://www.biogs.com/blair/. Accessed on February 20, 2011.

14. "Iraq War in Figures," BBC News, September 1, 2010, http://www.bbc.co.uk/news/world-middle-east-11107739. Accessed on March 31, 2011.

15. Alastair Finlan, *The Gulf War 1991*, 20.

16. John Keegan, *The Iraq War: The 21-Day Conflict and its Aftermath* (London: Pimlico, 2004), 129.

17. Alastair Finlan, *The Gulf War 1991*, 17.

18. John Keegan, *The Iraq War*, 128.

19. "The Battle for Umm Qasr," Britain's Small Wars, http://www.britains-smallwars.com/gulf2/UmmQasr.html. Accessed on February 20, 2011.

20. Bing West and Ray L. Smith, *The March Up: Taking Baghdad with the 1st Marine Division* (New York: Bantam Books, 2003).

21. "Saddam Statue Topples with Regime," BBC On This Day, April 9, 2003, http://news.bbc.co.uk/onthisday/hi/dates/stories/april/9/newsid_3502000/3502633.stm. Accessed on February 20, 2011.

22. "Saddam's Final Stronghold Crumbles," *The Guardian*, April 14, 2003, http://www.guardian.co.uk/world/2003/apr/14/iraq3. Accessed on February 20, 2011.

23. "Bush Calls End to 'major combat,'" CNN.com, May 2, 2003, http://edition.cnn.com/2003/WORLD/meast/05/01/sprj.irq.main/. Accessed on February 20, 2011.

24. John Simpson, *The Wars Against Saddam*, 320. "Baghdad International Airport [BIAP]," GlobalSecirity.org, http://www.globalsecurity.org/military/world/iraq/saddam-iap.htm. Accessed on February 20, 2011.

25. *Ibid.*

26. "Bodyguard Tells of Life on the Run," FOXNews.com, July 25, 2003, http://www.foxnews.com/story/0,2933,92911,00.html. Accessed on February 20, 2011.

27. "Looters Ransack Baghdad Museum," BBC News, April 12, 2003, http://news.bbc.co.uk/1/hi/world/middle_east/2942449.stm. Accessed on February 20, 2011.

28. Jane Warren, *The Ali Abbas Story: The Moving Story of One Boy's Struggle for Life* (London: Harper Collins, 2004).

Aftermath (pages 58–65)

1. "Iraq Invasion Plan 'delusional,'" BBC News, February 15, 2007, http://news.bbc.co.uk/1/hi/6364507.stm. Accessed on February 20, 2011.
2. "Up to 40 Die in Baghdad Attacks," *The Guardian*, October 27, 2003, http://www.guardian.co.uk/world/2003/oct/27/iraq. Accessed on February 20, 2011.
3. "Pentagon: Saddam's Sons Killed in Raid," CNN.com, July 23, 2003, http://edition.cnn.com/2003/WORLD/meast/07/22/sprj.irq.sons/index.html. Accessed on February 20, 2011.
4. "How Saddam Hussein Was Captured," BBC News, December 15, 2003, http://news.bbc.co.uk/1/hi/3317881.stm. Accessed on February 20, 2011.
5. "Baghdad: Mapping the Violence," *Iraq: Four Years On*, BBC News, http://news.bbc.co.uk/1/shared/spl/hi/in_depth/baghdad_navigator/. Accessed on February 20, 2011.
6. "Operation Vigilant Resolve," GlobalSecurity.org, http://www.globalsecurity.org/military/ops/oif-vigilant-resolve.htm. Accessed on February 20, 2011.
7. "Bodies Mutilated in Iraq Attack," BBC News, March 31, 2004, http://news.bbc.co.uk/1/hi/world/middle_east/3585765.stm. Accessed on February 20, 2011.
8. "Operation al-Fajr (Dawn): Operation Phantom Fury [Fallujah]," GlobalSecurity.org, http://www.globalsecurity.org/military/ops/oif-phantom-fury-fallujah.htm. Accessed on February 20, 2011.
9. *Ibid.*
10. Seymour M. Hersh, "Annals of National Security: Torture at Abu Ghraib," *New Yorker*, May 10, 2004, http://www.newyorker.com/archive/2004/05/10/040510fa_fact. Accessed on February 20, 2011.
11. "UK troops in Iraqi Torture Probe," BBC News, May 1, 2004, http://news.bbc.co.uk/1/hi/uk_politics/3675215.stm. Accessed on April 3, 2011; "British Soldiers Sexually Abused Us, Claim Iraqis," *The Independent*, November 15, 2009, http://www.independent.co.uk/news/uk/home-news/british-soldiers-sexually-abused-us-claim-iraqis-1820973.html. Accessed on April 3, 2011.
12. "Iraq Timeline," BBC News, http://news.bbc.co.uk/1/hi/world/middle_east/737483.stm. Accessed on February 20, 2011.
13. *Ibid.*
14. "U.S. Welcomes News That Iraqi Government Will Be Announced May 20," GlobalSecurity.org, May 17, 2006, http://www.globalsecurity.org/wmd/library/news/iraq/2006/05/iraq-060517-usia01.htm. Accessed on February 20, 2011.
15. "Profile: Blackwater USA," BBC News, October 8, 2007, http://news.bbc.co.uk/1/hi/7000645.stm. Accessed on February 20, 2011.
16. "Iraqi Blast Damages Shia Shrine," BBC News, February 22, 2006, http://news.bbc.co.uk/1/hi/world/middle_east/4738472.stm. Accessed on February 20, 2011.
17. "Decrying Violence in Iraq, UN Envoy Urges National Dialogue, International Support," UN News Center, November 25, 2006, http://www.un.org/apps/news/story.asp?NewsID=20726&Cr=Iraq&Cr1=. Accessed on February 20, 2011.

18. "Bush: 'We need to change our strategy in Iraq,'" CNN Politics, January 10, 2007, http://articles.cnn.com/2007-01-10/politics/bush.transcript_1_samarra-iraq-study-group-iraq-s-shia?_s=PM:POLITICS. Accessed on February 20, 2011.
19. "Pentagon: Violence Down in Iraq Since 'Surge,'" CNN World, June 23, 2008, http://articles.cnn.com/2008-06-23/world/iraq.security_1_troop-deaths-sadr-city-iraqi-troops?_s=PM:WORLD. Accessed on February 20, 2011.
20. *Ibid.*
21. Richard Norton-Taylor and Julian Borger, "The Battle for Basra: Iraqis Fight Mahdi Army as British Troops Remain at Base," *The Guardian*, March 26, 2008, http://www.guardian.co.uk/world/2008/mar/26/iraq.military. Accessed on February 20, 2011.
22. Kim Sengupta, "UK Troops Forced Out of Iraq as Mandate Expires," *The Independent*, July 29, 2009, http://www.independent.co.uk/news/world/middle-east/uk-troops-forced-out-of-iraq-as-mandate-expires-1764010.html. Accessed on February 20, 2011.
23. "Obama: U.S. to Withdraw Most Iraq Troops by August 2010," CNN, Politics, February 27, 2009, http://articles.cnn.com/2009-02-27/politics/obama.troops_1_iraq-troops-home-president-obama?_s=PM:POLITICS. Accessed on February 20, 2011.
24. Adam Gabbatt, "Last US Combat Troops Leave Iraq," *The Guardian*, August 19, 2010, http://www.guardian.co.uk/world/2010/aug/19/iraq-last-combat-troops-leave http://www.guardian.co.uk/world/2010/aug/19/iraq-last-combat-troops-leave. Accessed on February 20, 2011.
25. "Obama: U.S. to Withdraw Most Iraq Troops by August 2010," CNN.
26. Jessy Elmurr, "US Soldiers Returning from Iraq Face 'invisible wounds,'" BBC News US & Canada, August 30, 2010, http://www.bbc.co.uk/news/business/. Accessed on February 20, 2011.
27. John Donnelly, "More Troops Lost to Suicide," Congress.org, http://www.congress.org/news/2011/01/24/more_troops_lost_to_suicide. Accessed on June 13, 2011.
28. Gabriel Gatehouse, "'Normal life' in Iraq Amid the Violence," BBC News, December 20, 2010, http://www.bbc.co.uk/news/mobile/world-middle-east-12036265. Accessed on February 15, 2011.
29. "Decrying Violence in Iraq, UN Envoy Urges National Dialogue, International Support," UN News Center.
30. Martin Chulov, "The Children of Basra Learn to Live and Hope," *The Observer*, April 19, 2009, http://www.guardian.co.uk/world/2009/apr/19/children-basra-iraq-war-legacy. Accessed on February 15, 2011.

What Have We Learned? (pages 66–67)

1. Figures drawn from Alastair Finlan, *The Gulf War 1991*, 85, and Jack Kelly, "Estimates of Deaths in First War Still in Dispute," February 16, 2003, Post-Gazette.com, http://www.post-gazette.com/nation/20030216casualty0216p5.asp. Accessed on February 24, 2011 (an article comparing a range of sources for casualty figures in the First Gulf War).
2. Iraq Body Count, http://www.iraqbodycount.org/analysis/numbers/warlogs/. Accessed on February 24, 2011.

BIBLIOGRAPHY

Coughlin, Con. *Saddam: His Rise and Fall*. New York: Harper
 Perennial, 2005.

Finlan, Alastair. *Essential Histories: The Gulf War 1991*.
 Oxford: Osprey, 2003.

Keegan, John. *The Iraq War*. London: Hutchinson, 2004.

Lewis, Bernard. *The Middle East: 2000 Years of History
 from the Rise of Christianity to the Present Day*.
 London: Phoenix, 2000.

Ricks, Thomas E. *Fiasco: The American Adventure in Iraq*.
 New York: Penguin, 2007.

Ricks, Thomas E. *The Gamble*. New York: Penguin, 2010.

Salbi, Zainab, and Laurie Becklund. *Hidden in Plain Sight,
 Growing Up in the Shadow of Saddam*. London: Vision, 2005.

Simpson, John. *The Wars Against Saddam: Taking the
 Hard Road to Baghdad*. London: Macmillan, 2003.

Warren, Jane. *The Ali Abbas Story: The Moving Story of
 One Boy's Struggle for Life*. London: Harper Collins, 2004.

FIND OUT MORE

BOOKS

Carlisle, Rodney P., and John Stewart Bowman. *America at War: Iraq War.* New York: Chelsea House, 2010.

Ellis, Deborah. *Children of War: Voices of Iraq Refugees.* Toronto: House of Anansi, 2009.

Jaber, Hala. *The Flying Carpet of Small Miracles: A Woman's Fight to Save Two Orphans.* New York: Riverhead, 2009.

Mason, Paul. *Timelines: The Iraq War.* Mankato, Minn.: Arcturus, 2011.

Steele, Philip. *Eyewitness Guides: Ancient Iraq.* New York: Dorling Kindersley, 2007.

DOCUMENTARIES

Iraq's Lost Treasure (National Geographic, Archaeology Channel) To see this program, visit www.archaeologychannel.org/content/film/Lost-Treasure.htm.

The Iraq War: One Year Later (New York: A&E Entertainment, 2008)

WEBSITES

www.pbs.org/wgbh/pages/frontline/gulf/
Information about the First Gulf War can be found on this website of PBS.

http://edition.cnn.com/SPECIALS/2003/iraq/
The news channel CNN's website has lots of information about the Second Gulf War.

www.timeforkids.com/TFK/iraq
This website created by *Time* magazine has a variety of different features helping to explain the wars in Iraq, offering a variety of viewpoints.

INDEX